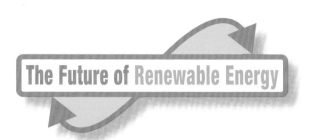

The Future of Renewable Energy

What Is the Future of Hydropower?

Stephen Currie

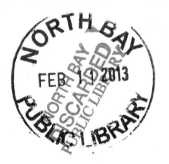

ReferencePoint
Press®

San Diego, CA

© 2013 ReferencePoint Press, Inc.
Printed in the United States

For more information, contact:
ReferencePoint Press, Inc.
PO Box 27779
San Diego, CA 92198
www.ReferencePointPress.com

Picture Credits:
Cover: Thinkstock.com
© China Photos/Reuters/Corbis: 8
Steve Zmina: 15, 20, 27, 34, 42, 47, 54, 59

LIBRARY OF CONGRESS CATALOGING-IN-PUBLICATION DATA

Currie, Stephen, 1960- author.
  What Is the Future of Hydropower?/by Stephen Currie.
    pages ; cm. -- (Future of renewable energy series)
  Audience: Grade 9-12
  Includes bibliographical references and index.
  ISBN-13: 978-1-60152-276-4 (hardback : alk. paper)
  ISBN-10: 1-60152-276-2 (hardback : alk. paper) 1. Water-power--Juvenile literature. I. Title.
  TC146.C87 2013
  333.91'4--dc23
                                                                                    2012020153

Contents

What are the long-term prospects for renewable energy?

In his 2011 State of the Union address, President Barack Obama set an ambitious goal for the United States: to generate 80 percent of its electricity from clean energy sources, including renewables such as wind, solar, biomass, and hydropower, by 2035. The president reaffirmed this goal in the March 2011 White House report *Blueprint for a Secure Energy Future*. The report emphasizes the president's view that continued advances in renewable energy are an essential piece of America's energy future. "Beyond our efforts to reduce our dependence on oil," the report states, "we must focus on expanding cleaner sources of electricity, including renewables like wind and solar, as well as clean coal, natural gas, and nuclear power—keeping America on the cutting edge of clean energy technology so that we can build a 21st century clean energy economy and win the future."

Obama's vision of America's energy future is not shared by all. Benjamin Zycher, a visiting scholar at the American Enterprise Institute, a conservative think tank, contends that policies aimed at shifting from conventional to renewable energy sources demonstrate a "disconnect between the rhetoric and the reality." In *Renewable Electricity Generation: Economic Analysis and Outlook* Zycher writes that renewables have inherent limitations that can be overcome only at a very high cost. He states: "Renewable electricity has only a small share of the market, and ongoing developments in the market for competitive fuels . . . make it likely that renewable electricity will continue to face severe constraints in terms of competitiveness for many years to come."

Is Obama's goal of 80 percent clean electricity by 2035 realistic? Expert opinions can be found on both sides of this question and on all of the other issues relating to the debate about what lies ahead for renewable energy. Driven by this reality, *The Future of Renewable Energy* series critically examines the long-term prospects for renewable energy by delving into the topics and opinions that dominate and inform renewable energy policy and debate. The series covers renewables such as solar, wind, biofuels, hydrogen, and hydropower and explores the issues of cost and affordability, impact on the environment, viability as a replacement for fossil fuels, and what role—if any—government should play in renewable energy development. Pointed questions (such as "Can Solar Power Ever Replace Fossil Fuels?" or "Should Government Play a Role in Developing Biofuels?") frame the discussion and support inquiry-based learning. The pro/con format of the series encourages critical analysis of the topics and opinions that shape the debate. Discussion in each book is supported by current and relevant facts and illustrations, quotes from experts, and real-world examples and anecdotes. Additionally, all titles include a list of useful facts, organizations to contact for further information, and other helpful sources for further reading and research.

Visions of the Future: Hydropower

In 1992 the government of China approved the building of a dam across the Yangtze River near the community of Sandouping, about 600 miles (1,000km) from the Pacific Ocean. The dam, intended mainly to generate electricity for China's growing economy, became known as the Three Gorges Dam—a reference to deep canyons and high bluffs in the surrounding region. Construction on the project began in 1994 and slowly took shape over the next decade or so. Part of the dam became operational in 2006, but much of the project still remained unfinished at that point. Indeed, as of early 2012, nearly 20 years after it was begun, the Three Gorges project is not yet officially complete.

As the time line of the project suggests, the Three Gorges Dam was—and is—a massive undertaking. "It is the largest engineering project on the face of the earth,"[1] a journalist reported in 1996, soon after construction got under way. Upon completion, the dam will be over 7,600 feet (2,330m) long, a distance of well over a mile. Its height will be nearly 600 feet (183m). Thus far, building the dam has required over 35 million cubic yards (27 million cubic meters) of concrete and more than 60 times the amount of steel used in the Eiffel Tower. On the basis of size alone, the dam is often referred to by tour operators and other observers as the "eighth wonder of the world."[2]

The primary purpose of the Three Gorges Dam is to produce hydropower, or electricity from the energy contained in moving water. The principles behind hydropower are simple. As rivers flow from higher places to lower places, they carry energy. The faster they travel and the quicker they descend, the more energy they have. By anchoring wooden wheels and other devices in places where river currents will move them, people can harness this energy and use it for their own purposes. Indeed, hydropower dates back many centuries. Cultures that made use of hydropower for grinding grain or other purposes include the ancient Greeks, the early Egyptians, and the ancient Chinese.

Over time, the process of tapping rivers for power has steadily become more sophisticated. By building dams to hold back the river, engineers can increase the distance the water must fall, thereby adding to the energy it carries. The wooden wheels of the ancients, too, have been replaced by more technologically complex equipment. At Three Gorges, as at most large dams around the world, water flows past a series of turbines—steel devices that spin rapidly when water strikes them. That spinning transfers energy from the river to an electrical generator in the dam or on the riverbank nearby. The generator converts the water power to electricity, which can be stored or sent out for immediate use.

Energy Production

The electrical output of hydropower plants is usually measured in units called *megawatts*, a single megawatt being equal to 1 million watts. The exact amount of energy a hydropower plant produces will vary according to water levels, the effectiveness of the turbines, and other factors. Still, engineers can predict roughly how many watts any given hydropower plant will generate. This figure is called the dam's capacity. A small dam might have a capacity of 10–20 megawatts, while larger installations could produce several hundred megawatts. Extremely large hydroelectric complexes can generate even more—over 6,000 megawatts in the case of the Grand Coulee Dam on the Columbia River in Washington, the largest hydropower facility in the United States.

These figures are impressive. But they are dwarfed by the amount of energy produced by the Three Gorges Dam. Though it is still unfinished, this dam already has a capacity of about 20,000 megawatts—three times the generating power of Grand Coulee and enough to provide electrical power to over 20 million households. Upon its completion, moreover,

Dam construction is a huge and expensive undertaking, as it has been with China's Three Gorges Dam (pictured), and it is not free of human or environmental costs. But the enormous amount of power that dams such as this one provide suggests the significance of hydropower as a future source of energy.

the capacity of the Three Gorges project is expected to rise to roughly 22,500 megawatts. That is half again the capacity of its closest competitor, a hydroelectric plant at the Itaipu Dam on the border between Brazil and Paraguay. Both today and in the immediate future the Three Gorges Dam stands by itself where hydropower capacity is concerned.

Certainly, China needs all the electricity the Three Gorges project can provide. After increasing slowly from the 1970s to the 1990s, China's overall energy consumption suddenly skyrocketed. Between 2002 and 2009 alone, China's energy use per person nearly doubled—and given the needs of China's growing economy and increasingly influential middle class, projections indicate that energy use in China will continue to rise sharply through the foreseeable future. The addition of 20,000 or more megawatts through the Three Gorges Dam, though it is not nearly enough to solve all of China's energy concerns, will help meet that demand.

Production and Advantages

The enormous amount of power that the completed Three Gorges project will provide suggests not only that hydroelectricity is an important piece of energy production today but also that waterpower will be even more significant in the future. In some ways, this view is correct. Today, hydropower accounts for about 20 percent of the world's electricity needs, giving it an important role in the mix of energy sources used by people across the globe. And the success of the Three Gorges project has sparked interest in building even larger dams in other nations. The proposed Grand Inga project in the Democratic Republic of the Congo, for example, would generate 39,000 megawatts of electricity, dwarfing even the amount produced by the Three Gorges Dam.

As a source of power, moreover, hydroelectricity has several distinct advantages. One is the cost of the energy it produces. As with other major hydroelectric projects around the world, the Three Gorges project generates power at a relatively low cost. As long as the Yangtze River flows normally, capturing the power from the dam is easy. In contrast, supplies of fuels such as coal—which to date has produced most of China's electricity—must be constantly replenished, adding to the price of the power it generates. Most reports suggest that when the dam is complete, the electricity it produces will be available for less money than electricity produced by other means.

Likewise, because hydropower does not require burning, hydroelectric facilities are not as harmful to the environment as plants that run on coal or similar fuels. Indeed, hydropower is notable because it produces virtually no air pollution or carbon dioxide—a greenhouse gas associated with climate change, given off when fuels such as coal and oil are burned. Instead of building the Three Gorges complex, China could have chosen to generate the same amount of energy by constructing more coal-fired plants. That might have been a problematic choice, however. According to one estimate, every year the extra coal plants would have produced an additional "100 million tons of carbon dioxide, 1.2–2 million tons of sulfur dioxide, 10,000 tons of carbon monoxide, and large quantities of particulates"[3]—all of which were avoided by the decision to construct the Three Gorges project instead.

Disadvantages

At the same time, Three Gorges also points out several significant drawbacks to hydroelectricity—drawbacks that suggest to many observers that waterpower may not play an especially important role in the energy world of the future after all. Though the Three Gorges facility may produce relatively cheap electricity, for instance, the cost to construct the dam is staggering. Officially, China will spend between $22 and $27 billion to build the entire facility; but many outside observers believe that the true cost is significantly higher even than that. It is not at all clear whether poorer countries can afford these massive expenditures.

The Three Gorges project has raised other difficult questions, too. Even though the facility does not cause air pollution, it is not as environmentally friendly as the Chinese government originally suggested. The reservoir created by the dam flooded hundreds of square miles, destroying habitat and endangering several species of plants and animals. Water pollution has been a problem too, and some experts warn that the sheer weight of the dam could cause earthquakes. Even government officials are finally beginning to recognize the environmental problems. "We must strengthen ecological protection and control pollution in the reservoir area," reads an official statement issued in 2011.[4]

An Uncertain Future

The Three Gorges Dam, then, highlights both the best and the worst of hydropower. On the one hand, the dam creates electricity needed to strengthen the Chinese economy, and the electricity it generates is less expensive and less environmentally destructive than electricity generated from fuels such as coal. On the other hand, the overall cost of the project has been massive, and the dam has caused environmental and other concerns that cannot be easily dismissed. How—and whether—these contradictions can be resolved will go a long way toward determining the role that hydropower will play as an energy source in the future.

Chapter One

Can Hydropower Ever Replace Fossil Fuels?

Hydropower Can Help Replace Fossil Fuels

Clean, cheap, and reliable, hydropower has several important advantages over fossil fuels as a source of energy for human use. To date, however, hydropower resources have not been developed to their fullest. Many countries have rivers that are ideal for hydroelectric production yet have never been tapped. Technological innovation, too, can help produce machines such as electricity-powered cars, which can make better use of the low-cost, renewable resource of hydroelectric power. As traditional fossil fuels drop in availability and rise in price, hydropower will prove an important source of energy for future generations.

The Debate

Hydropower Cannot Replace Fossil Fuels

Hydropower is no substitute for oil, coal, and natural gas. While hydropower is very good at producing electricity, it cannot easily be transformed into substitutes for gasoline or heating oil. There are also questions about how much more electricity hydropower can realistically produce. Many parts of the world are too flat or too dry to benefit much from hydropower; in some places, too, the best rivers have already been tapped near their capacity. Add questions about cost, the environment, and other issues, and it is evident that hydropower can never actually replace oil, coal, and gas.

Hydropower Can Help Replace Fossil Fuels

"Hydropower is the only renewable source of energy that can replace fossil fuels' electricity production while satisfying growing energy needs."

— Agriculture and Rural Development of Alberta, Canada, which oversees Alberta's agriculture and food industries.

Government of Alberta [Canada], Agriculture and Rural Development, "Hydroelectric Power," May 27, 2010. www1.agric.gov.ab.ca.

Although hydropower is an inexpensive and environmentally friendly form of energy, it is often overlooked as an energy source. In particular, hydroelectricity can be overshadowed by the widespread use of fossil fuels such as oil, coal, and natural gas. In today's society, these materials account for over 85 percent of the world's total energy production. Because of fossil fuels' importance, coal, natural gas, and oil are a main focus of energy planners, power companies, and the general public. The news is full of information about rising gasoline prices and concerns about natural gas supplies. News stories about hydropower, in contrast, are more difficult to find.

At the same time, however, hydropower is also discounted by many people whose interest lies in nontraditional fuel sources. In particular, hydropower is typically ignored in favor of wind and solar energy. In the popular mind, these two forms of energy are nearly synonymous with terms like *renewable energy* and *green power*. Certainly each has attracted a great deal of attention in the modern world. Indeed, both solar and wind power are routinely described as fashionable, up-and-coming sources of energy. One energy corporation refers to wind power as "the trendy energy alternative,"[5] for example, and another describes solar energy as "hip [and] cool."[6] Few observers describe hydropower in similar terms.

12

Despite the lack of attention it receives, hydroelectricity is nonetheless an important source of energy in today's world. Already, an estimated 20 percent of the globe's electricity is generated from hydroelectric plants. In some countries, notably Norway and Paraguay, virtually all electricity comes from hydropower. In other nations, including Brazil and Canada, hydropower accounts for over half the electricity produced. And even in the United States, where just 6 percent of the electricity is obtained from hydroelectric plants, hydropower makes up an important share of electricity production in states such as Oregon, New York, and Idaho. Without hydropower, the world would have less energy and would pay more for it.

In the future, moreover, hydropower's importance is almost certain to rise. One reason is simply that fossil fuels will not last forever. Most current estimates suggest that about half the world's oil supplies have already been used up, with significant amounts of the remainder locked away in places where it is difficult to reach—and may not be cost-effective to recover. Moreover, global demand for oil and other fossil fuels has skyrocketed in recent years, in large part because of the growing economies of high-population countries such as India and China. The result is that the world's supplies of oil, coal, and natural gas are being depleted at an ever increasing rate—and someday will run out altogether.

> **"Most renewable technologies other than hydroelectricity are not able to compete economically with fossil fuels."[9]**
>
> —US Energy Information Administration.

The Need for Alternatives

Some energy experts argue that the world is already feeling the effects of a dwindling supply of fossil fuels. One natural result of a declining supply is a rise in cost. As fossil fuels become scarcer and more in demand, it makes sense that their cost would increase—as indeed it has been doing in recent years. "As the 20th century turned into the 21st century," notes energy analyst Samuel R. Avro, "gas prices began to spike at an incredible rate . . . an astronomical 243 percent rise in under 15 years."[7] This increase in price, Avro adds, is several times the rate of inflation. This price jump has several contributing factors, but one important cause is simply that fossil fuels are becoming more difficult to find and more costly to produce.

A few scientists play down concerns about dwindling supply. They believe that there are vast unknown oil fields that will someday be found and tapped. These fields, they argue, will provide enough oil for many years to come. Other experts, however, scoff at this optimistic perspective. "Better to believe in the tooth fairy," writes author and scientist David Goodstein. Like many other scientists today, Goodstein suspects that the world's supply of fossil fuels may run out considerably before 2100. Given the current reliance on coal, gas, and oil in today's society, that spells disaster. As Goodstein warns, "Civilization as we know it will come to an end sometime in this century unless we can find a way to live without fossil fuels."[8]

The task for humanity, then, is to find alternatives to fossil fuel use—and to find them quickly. Because time is limited, these alternative fuels are most likely to be energy sources already in use today. The advantages of hydropower put it at the top of the list. As one example, hydropower is more reliable than wind energy and solar power, which are highly dependent on weather conditions. Similarly, as nuclear disasters in Japan and the former Soviet Union have demonstrated, nuclear power plants carry enormous risks to the environment. Whatever its flaws, hydropower will never release radioactivity into the surrounding area.

Expense and Growth

Hydropower's most important advantage over other alternative fuels, however, is economic. Hydroelectricity is cheaper at present than most other forms of energy and likely to remain so. The US Energy Information Administration, for example, projects that hydropower will be among the least expensive sources of electricity for the United States in 2016, considerably ahead of solar-generated electricity and comfortably outperforming nuclear and wind as well. "Most renewable technologies other than hydroelectricity are not able to compete economically with fossil fuels,"[9] notes the agency. As time goes on and the price of fossil fuels continues to rise, the disparity between the cost of hydropower and the cost of virtually all other sources will continue to grow.

Projected Growth in Hydropower Capacity Through 2035

The Energy Information Administration, an agency of the US government, predicts a steady increase in the world's hydropower capacity over the next 2 decades. With this projected increase, hydropower will be able to fill more and more of the world's energy needs. This graph uses data taken from the EIA's 2011 Annual Energy Outlook report. It shows the world's actual hydroelectric generating capacity in 2010, and then gives the agency's best guesses about how that capacity will change through 2035. The vertical axis shows the number of gigawatts produced; 1 gigawatt is equal to 1 billion watts or 1,000 megawatts. The graph predicts an average growth rate of about 2 percent a year.

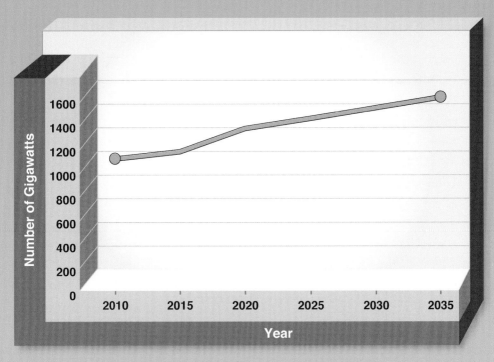

Hydropower is well positioned to replace fossil fuels for other reasons, too. One is that the world's production of hydroelectricity is significantly under its capacity. China, for example, produces less than 20 percent of its electricity from hydropower, a figure that puts it near the world average. However, China has plenty of untapped rivers that will someday provide a great deal of energy. Seeing the value of hydroelectricity in today's world, the Chinese government has embarked on a large-scale program to increase its hydroelectric capacity. Chinese officials expect that by 2020, about 70 percent of the nation's electricity will come from hydropower.

The underutilization of waterpower is especially true in the developing world. At present, the nations of southern and central Africa together tap only an estimated 5 percent of their full hydropower potential. Many large rivers remain virtually untapped, and existing hydroelectric dams typically produce much less energy than they can. The hydropower plants built along central Africa's Congo River, for example, already produce a few thousand megawatts of electricity, but the river could generate tens of thousands more megawatts if new dams were built in the appropriate places.

Indeed, several new power plants in Africa and other parts of the developing world are already under construction. The Gilgel Gibe III Dam in Ethiopia, for example, is scheduled for completion in 2013, though delays may postpone the opening date. Once finished, the dam is expected to produce nearly 2,000 megawatts of electricity, more than doubling Ethiopia's current hydropower production. Other hydroelectric plants are still in the planning stages. The most impressive of these, Grand Inga Dam in the Democratic Republic of the Congo, would have a capacity of 39,000 megawatts, making it the largest dam in the world. Projects are also under consideration or being built in parts of South America and central and southeastern Asia.

More Electricity

Unlike in the developing world, many of the rivers of Europe and the United States have been tapped to near their capacity. Even in these places, however, hydropower has room to grow. The Department of Energy

(DOE) has identified well over 100,000 sites around the United States that could be used to generate hydroelectricity. Although many of these sites can support only relatively small power stations, the combined effect of dozens or hundreds of small power facilities can be significant. "The [United States] could be producing 13,000 megawatts of power from hydrokinetic energy [hydroelectricity] by 2025," reports the Union of Concerned Scientists, an organization of scientists who advocate for environmental issues. "This level of development is equivalent to displacing 22 new dirty coal-fired power plants."[10] The DOE, similarly, estimates that the United States could easily produce an extra 30,000 megawatts a year from hydroelectricity.

Hydropower does have its limits as a fuel source. In particular, the energy of water is difficult to transfer into forms other than electricity. Thus, hydropower cannot easily be used for gasoline and other similar products. Nonetheless, technological changes can make hydropower more important than it is at present. Though nearly all cars in the early twenty-first century run exclusively on gasoline, for example, the future for electricity-powered vehicles is bright. In the United States, the fledgling electric car industry sold over 30,000 vehicles in 2011, and demand for these vehicles increased in early 2012. Other technological breakthroughs can likewise make hydroelectricity more widely useful.

> "The [United States] could be producing 13,000 megawatts of power from hydrokinetic energy [hydroelectricity] by 2025."[10]
>
> —Union of Concerned Scientists.

No one argues that hydropower is the only answer to the world's energy troubles. Nor does anyone believe that it is the sole power source that can replace fossil fuels. Still, it is clear that hydropower can play an important role in replacing fossil fuels. More than most other energy sources, its cleanliness, cost, and dependability make it an excellent candidate for greater use in the future.

Hydropower Cannot Replace Fossil Fuels

"Renewable energy [including hydropower] currently makes up less than 2% of the world's primary energy supply, and although growing very rapidly, it is not on course to fill the fossil fuel gap."

—Chris Nelder, an author who writes about the energy industry and energy issues.

Chris Nelder, "The End of Fossil Fuel," *Forbes*, July 24, 2009.

The era of fossil fuels is coming to an end. No matter how many undiscovered oil fields and natural gas reserves there may still be, the globe's fossil fuel supplies will one day be exhausted. Before then, the people of the world will need a plan for replacing that energy. Otherwise, the world risks catastrophe as the power it relies on for commerce, communication, and transport gradually disappears. "There is a growing consensus that we must replace fossil fuels with renewable sources of energy," notes energy writer Brian Somers, "and fast."[11]

Fortunately, there are a number of ways to make up for the diminishing supply of fossil fuels. Unfortunately, hydropower is not among them. While hydroelectric production, like any source of energy, can help meet a few of the world's power needs, it is unrealistic to believe that hydroelectricity could begin to replace fossil fuels. Hydropower has too many limitations to allow it to take the place of coal, oil, and gas—or, for that matter, to provide more than a small fraction of the energy currently supplied by these fossil fuels. If the world is to replace fossil fuels, it will need to turn to resources that are cheaper, more flexible, and more widely available than hydropower. As the leaders of a renewable energy corporation put it, "While hydropower has not come to an end, it's clearly not destined to supplant coal and natural gas power plants in any major capacity."[12]

Geography and Weather

One of the most significant problems with hydropower involves geography. Hilly, wet parts of the world are best suited for hydropower generation. According to a Scandinavian energy agency, for example, the rugged mountains and high precipitation of Norway and Sweden give these countries "the ideal conditions for producing hydropower."[13] Not surprisingly, then, these countries are among the leaders in generating hydroelectricity. Other places with the right conditions to produce hydropower include Japan, Paraguay, and the US states of Washington, Oregon, and Idaho. Like Norway and Sweden, these places also rank high on the list of states and nations that generate hydroelectricity.

But if some landscapes and weather conditions support hydropower production, many others do not. For the most part, areas that receive little rainfall are not good candidates for hydroelectric plants; there is simply not enough water to make hydropower a significant source of energy. The Arabian peninsula, for example, is extremely dry, with some regions experiencing no rainfall over a period of several years; not surprisingly, the peninsula derives virtually no energy from hydropower. Likewise, it is difficult to produce hydroelectricity in flat territory, where rivers typically move slowly and gravity is seldom a factor. Though Mississippi and Florida get plenty of rain, their low elevations mean that hydropower can be at best a negligible source of their electricity.

The result is that wide stretches of the earth's surface are unsuitable for hydroelectricity. To make matters worse, in many parts of the world where it is feasible, hydroelectricity is already being tapped to near its capacity. Along rivers where a large number of dams are already in place, adding new dams rarely increases energy production: No good sites remain. In much of Europe and the United States, as a result, energy companies already harness 75 percent or more of rivers' available power. There is not enough unused capacity to allow hydropower to provide much more of the developed world's energy.

"While hydropower has not come to an end, it's clearly not destined to supplant coal and natural gas power plants in any major capacity."[12]

—Ecoleaf, a company involved in developing clean energy.

Hydropower Production by State, 2010

Hydroelectric capacity in the United States is limited to certain parts of the country, which shows that hydropower is not a realistic way to fulfill the nation's energy needs. This map groups the states according to how much hydropower they produced in 2010. The 8 states shaded green or blue each produce over 7.5 million megawatt-hours of hydroelectricity a year, enough to account for a significant share of the state's electrical generation. Each of the remaining 42 states (shaded yellow) produces fewer than 7.5 million megawatt-hours of electricity from hydropower. In most cases, the electricity produced from hydropower in these states is considerably below this figure. As a rule, these states are simply too flat or too dry to make much use of hydroelectricity.

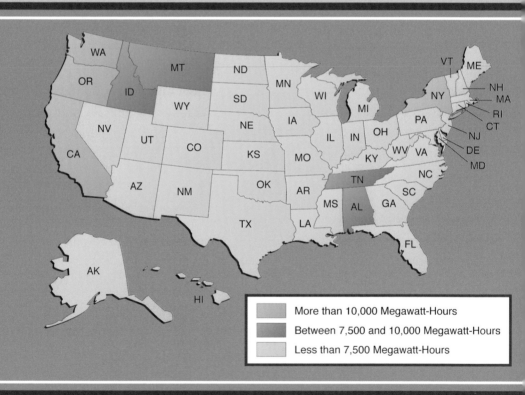

More than 10,000 Megawatt-Hours

Between 7,500 and 10,000 Megawatt-Hours

Less than 7,500 Megawatt-Hours

Source: US Energy Information Administration, "Renewable and Alternative Fuels: Hydroelectric, Net Generation from Hydroelectric (Conventional) Power by State by Sector, Year-to-Date Through December 2010 and 2009," 2010. www.eia.gov.

Fewer Dams, Lower Capacity

Neither does there seem to be much interest at present in constructing new hydropower plants within the United States. As of 2012 the United States had very few large hydroelectric projects in the planning stages, and it is not clear that any of these few will actually be built. The largest of these projects, the Susitna Dam in Alaska, would cost over $4 billion to build and has been actively opposed by a number of groups concerned about the dam's costs and its potential effect on the ecology of the region. The Alaska Center for the Environment, for example, refers to the project as Alaska's "very own mega-dam boondoggle."[14] Even if the dam is eventually completed, construction is expected to take 10 years or more. The extremely slow pace of hydropower development in the United States makes it difficult to see how hydroelectricity can ever supplant fossil fuels as a major source of American energy.

In fact, current rates of hydropower production in parts of the developed world may turn out to be unsustainably high. Rising global temperatures are already leading to changes in the amount of water carried by rivers. The main culprits to date are melting glaciers and altered patterns of rainfall. In several parts of South America, rivers routinely carry less water than they did a decade or two ago. Water levels have diminished, for example, in both the Chubut River in Argentina and the Paraná River in Paraguay and Brazil. As a result of the lower water levels, river flows are less powerful, and less electricity can be produced by hydropower plants along these rivers.

Nor is the problem limited to South America. Angola, Namibia, South Africa, and Nigeria are among the African nations in which water levels in important rivers have dropped; several of these countries rely heavily on hydropower for their electricity. As for Europe, one recent study suggests that by 2035 Switzerland may lose up to 25 percent of its present hydroelectric generating capacity. As environmental writer Kristin Underwood puts it, "Countries that have built dams as part of their 'clean' energy future may have to rethink that future, thanks to climate change. As glaciers are melting faster and faster, the water just isn't there."[15]

Hydropower production could be increased in parts of the developing world, where plenty of rivers remain untapped. But it is unwise to assume that generating more hydroelectricity in the developing world will add much to the world's energy supply. One reason is the uncertainty that power plants along these rivers will ever be built. The costs of constructing large dams can run well into the billions of dollars, often far beyond the financial resources of small, poor countries. Developing nations such as Ethiopia and Bangladesh, for example, have announced plans to build extensive hydroelectric facilities in the past, only to delay those plans indefinitely while officials seek out the financing to make the project a reality.

And even if all of these proposed dams were actually constructed, it is uncertain how much energy they can ultimately provide. Though some of the hydropower plants planned for developing countries could produce tens of thousands of megawatts of electricity, even this amounts to a tiny proportion of the world's energy needs. The United States alone uses nearly 4 billion megawatts of electricity each year. It is simply unrealistic to expect that the world's energy needs will be met by damming all the rivers of Africa—or any other part of the globe.

Ecology, People, and Flexibility

The notion that hydropower can someday supplant fossil fuels is problematic for other reasons, too. When a dam is built, large stretches of land are permanently flooded. This flooding often causes environmental problems. In some areas species have been wiped out altogether after a dam has been constructed. In others the quality of the water has been negatively affected, causing problems for fish, birds, and plants. Large dams can even produce methane, a greenhouse gas that contributes to climate change. As environmental awareness grows, especially in the developed world, the ecological effects of hydroelectricity will likely dissuade some investors and power companies from championing hydropower as a solution to the world's energy problems.

The floods caused by dam construction also displace people, most notably in developing countries. In 2000 an international organization called the World Commission on Dams concluded that dam construction—most of it for hydroelectric purposes—had displaced at least 40 million people worldwide, possibly many more. "Most of these people have never regained their former livelihoods,"[16] the report adds. Observers agree that the displacement of people has continued steadily since the report was issued, with the same unfortunate results. Building a dam, then, carries with it a significant human cost—a cost that may dampen enthusiasm for hydropower in the future.

An even bigger drawback to hydropower is its lack of flexibility. Though running water can be turned into electric power, it cannot be transformed into gasoline or most other forms of fuel. Until and unless most vehicles and heating systems are powered by electricity, then, reliance on hydropower will leave a gap that cannot be filled. The time when everything is electric, however, is a long way off—and indeed may never arrive. Despite heavy government subsidies in some places, to say nothing of a great many glowing news and opinion articles about new technologies, electric cars remain extremely rare, and projections indicate that they are not gaining rapidly in popularity. In 2009 London mayor Boris Johnson promised that 100,000 electric vehicles would be on city streets "as soon as possible."[17] In the ensuing three years, however, only a few hundred electric vehicles have been registered in the city. As of early 2012 less than one-tenth of one percent of London's cars ran on electricity—and the number seems unlikely to increase significantly during the next few years.

It would be comforting to believe that hydropower could fully—or even mostly—replace the world's current addiction to fossil fuels. But that is out of the question. Inflexible, costly, environmentally problematic, and geographically limited, hydropower will never be more than a small contributor to the world's energy supply.

> "Countries that have built dams as part of their 'clean' energy future may have to rethink that future, thanks to climate change. As glaciers are melting faster and faster, the water just isn't there."[15]
>
> —Environmental writer Kristin Underwood.

Chapter Two

Is Hydropower Affordable?

Hydropower Is an Inexpensive Source of Fuel

Hydropower can be a cheap and plentiful source of fuel. In places where hydroelectricity is widely available, consumers usually pay less for power than they do elsewhere. This is in part because hydropower is a renewable energy source. Moreover, costs associated with labor, transportation, and similar expenses are low for hydropower compared to oil and other fossil fuels. Once the equipment to tap the energy of a body of water is in place, it costs relatively little to convert that energy into usable fuel. From an economic perspective, this makes hydropower a good choice for the future.

The Debate

Hydropower Is Much More Expensive than It Appears

Though the costs of running a hydropower plant are relatively low, the cost of building a hydroelectric facility is enormous. A hydroelectric facility of almost any size can be expected to cost in the hundreds of millions of dollars. Building a dam, constructing a power plant, adding to existing power grids—all are expensive. Few governments and private enterprises have the funds necessary to take on such massive projects. These huge price tags need to be factored into the cost of hydroelectricity—making it a less attractive option from an economic point of view.

Hydropower Is an Inexpensive Source of Fuel

"Hydropower is the cheapest and cleanest source of energy."

—Scott Tipton, US representative from Colorado.

Quoted in Troy Hooper, "Controversial Hydropower Bill Passes House," *Colorado Independent*, March 7, 2012. http://coloradoindependent.com.

Electricity prices vary considerably across the United States. During 2010, the most recent year for which figures are available, the average cost for one kilowatt-hour of electricity—that is, the amount of energy needed to power a 1,000-watt device for one hour—varied from around six cents in some states to 25 cents in Hawaii. A number of factors affect the cost of energy in any given state, but one notable influence is the amount of electricity that the state produces from hydropower. Idaho, for example, boasts the lowest electrical rates in the nation—customers in that state paid just over six cents per kilowatt-hour in 2010—and Idaho generates virtually all its electricity from hydropower. Washington, similarly, produces more hydroelectricity than any other state—and has the third lowest electric costs in the country.

The connection between low electric rates and hydropower production is not limited to the United States. Some of the lowest electrical rates in the world are in countries where hydropower production thrives. Paraguay, for example, produces virtually all its electricity from hydropower, notably from the Itaipu Dam across the Paraná River on the country's border with Brazil. Paraguay also has extremely cheap electricity. Residential customers pay the equivalent of about six US cents per kilowatt-hour, less than half the cost in nearby South American nations such as Chile and Uruguay.

The link is clear: Places that rely on hydropower production often have lower electrical rates than places that do not. There are exceptions, of course. Some countries that produce a great deal of oil, for instance, also have low electricity costs despite generating little or no hydroelectricity. But for the most part the connection between low electrical rates and hydropower generation is real—and far from a coincidence. Hydropower is a cheap form of energy, one of the cheapest available today. Places like Idaho and Paraguay enjoy low electricity prices in large part because so much of their energy comes from hydropower.

Reliable and Renewable

Hydropower is cheap for a number of reasons. One of these involves the renewability of water. When oil, coal, or natural gas are burned to create heat and light, those fossil fuels are destroyed forever. To continue to produce power from these materials requires getting more of them, and getting more requires plenty of money. Oil must be pumped up from hidden reservoirs; coal must be dug out from under the ground. The labor costs involved in obtaining these resources are enormous. Then the raw materials must be transported to refineries and power plants—an expensive proposition as well. The cost of transportation makes up close to 20 percent of the price of coal, for example.

In comparison, the water that flows past hydroelectric turbines is continually replenished. No one needs to locate a new water supply once one day's flow has been converted to electricity. Nor is it necessary to transport the water from one place to another. By eliminating the need to dig up fuels and transport them long distances, hydropower avoids significant costs invariably associated with electrical production from fossil fuel sources. And because electricity from hydropower costs less to produce, it can usually be sold for less.

The reliability of hydropower also helps make it an inexpensive source of electricity. Though the water level in rivers does fluctuate according to the amount of rainfall and the time of year, the volume and speed of river water is usually enough to produce a steady supply of energy. Except in times of extreme drought or in cases when emergency maintenance is

26

The Projected Cost of Hydropower Compared with Other Energy Sources

Hydropower is currently one of the cheapest available energy sources. The US Energy Information Administration uses a metric called *levelized cost* to compare the costs of different fuel sources. Levelized cost includes the actual cost of power generation, along with other factors such as the capital cost of building the power plant. This chart gives the levelized costs of six different energy sources used in the United States. The information is given for power plants that would open in 2016, and the costs are national averages. The lower the levelized cost of a given energy source, the less expensive the energy will be.

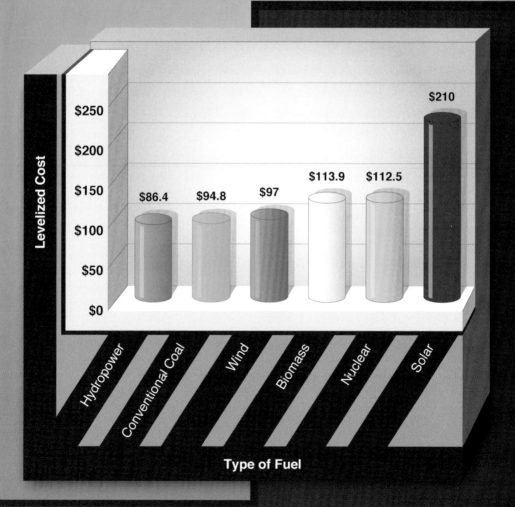

Source: US Energy Information Administration, *Levelized Cost of New Generation Resources in the Annual Energy Outlook 2011*, November 2010.

needed, the supply of hydroelectricity is rarely much affected from one day to the next, let alone from one month or year to another. Because the amount of energy produced by a hydroelectric plant is predictable, the cost is therefore predictable as well.

This stability in both supply and price is standard for hydropower. For technological and economic reasons, however, most other forms of energy do not enjoy this advantage. Oil, for example, is prone to sudden price hikes as the world's available supply varies—and as oil companies and governments react to political developments in oil-producing countries. It is not unusual for oil prices to rise substantially within the space of several days. In February 2011, for example, oil prices rose almost 10 percent in one week, the result of political unrest in North Africa and the Middle East. Outright warfare in oil-exporting nations would have an even more dramatic effect on oil availability and price. In early 2012, for instance, energy and political analysts warned that oil prices would spike if the United States were to become involved in a war with Iran.

The steady supply and price of hydroelectric power also represents an improvement over several renewable energy sources. Solar power is one example. As one British politician notes, "You need the electricity [even] when the sun doesn't shine"[18]—but at present it is difficult to store solar energy for later use. Wind power is another example. During a period of low wind, wind turbines sit idle, and electricity becomes both less available and more expensive. Again, this is in sharp contrast with hydropower.

Efficiency and Price Stability

Efficiency is another reason why hydropower makes sense economically. No power plant is able to convert all the energy in any given substance into usable power for human use. When fossil fuels are burned, for example, only about half the power in the original fuel is captured for human use. The rest is lost. Most experts agree that this situation will not change any time soon. Water turbines, in contrast, represent a much more effective way to convert the power of nature into electricity. "Hydropower is the most efficient way to generate electricity," reports a corporation that manages dams and reservoirs along the Wisconsin River. "Modern hydro turbines can convert as much as 90% of the available energy into electricity."[19] The more efficiently the energy can be converted, the cheaper the cost to consumers.

Hydropower plants, even small ones, are expensive to build. A small hydropower plant proposed for the South American country of Guyana, for example, is expected to cost between $500 million and $600 million; a somewhat larger dam complex planned for a river in Turkey may cost $1.6 billion. These costs are a concern, especially because they are typically about twice as high as the cost of building a similarly-sized plant that uses fossil fuels. Still, the inexpensiveness of hydroelectricity often makes up for the heavy initial costs. "Every year," notes an engineer, hydropower plants in Pakistan "pay back three times their original cost by generating [cheap] hydroelectricity."[20] These savings, moreover, mount up over a long period of time. Large hydroelectric plants built today, after all, are expected to remain in use for up to a century.

> **"Modern hydro turbines can convert as much as 90% of the available energy into electricity."[19]**
>
> —Wisconsin Valley Improvement Company.

Where costs are concerned, moreover, the future of hydropower may prove even more appealing than it is now. One reason is the gloomy outlook for fossil fuels. Nearly all experts agree that over time these fuels will become scarcer and more expensive. "By the end of this century," notes energy writer Chris Nelder, "nearly all the recoverable fossil fuels will be gone."[21] But as the costs of oil and gas rise, the price of hydropower is expected to remain steady. Since hydroelectricity is a renewable form of energy, there is no reason to expect its cost to rise. Even if power from water is relatively more expensive today than power made from fossil fuels, that will not be the case in the future.

Government Support

Another reason for the brighter financial outlook for hydroelectricity is the increasing involvement of governments in building and maintaining waterpower plants. With several important exceptions, such as China

29

and Paraguay, governments have typically provided much more funding for power plants that make use of fossil fuels than for plants that make use of renewables. In 2010, for instance, governments worldwide spent $409 billion on subsidies for fossil fuel technology, compared to only about $66 billion in support for renewable energy of all kinds. Given the environmental issues with fossil fuels, not to mention the fact that they will eventually give out altogether, the heavy subsidies for coal, gas, and oil make little sense. "Energy markets can be thought of as suffering from appendicitis due to fossil fuel subsidies," writes economist Fatih Birol, who adds that fossil fuel subsidies are "undermining the competitiveness of renewables."[22]

> "We've subsidized oil companies for a century. That's long enough. It's time to [support] a clean energy industry. . . . Pass clean energy tax credits. Create these jobs."[23]
>
> —Barack Obama, forty-fourth president of the United States.

There are signs that governments are beginning to rethink their funding of fossil fuels at the expense of hydropower and other renewables. In his State of the Union address of early 2012, for example, US president Barack Obama spoke out forcefully for a new way of thinking about energy subsidies. "We've subsidized oil companies for a century," Obama said. "That's long enough. It's time to [support] a clean energy industry. . . . Pass clean energy tax credits. Create these jobs."[23] Whether the US government will act on Obama's initiatives remains to be seen. Nonetheless, the movement in much of the world is toward larger subsidies for hydroelectricity and other forms of renewable energy. Such changes can only make hydropower cheaper for customers and provide funding for scientists to increase energy production through waterpower. The result, increasingly, will be to make hydropower a better, less expensive fuel.

Hydropower Is Much More Expensive than It Appears

"Actual costs for hydropower dams are almost always far higher than estimated; in a number of cases, the actual cost [is] more than double the estimated cost."

—International Rivers, an organization that works to protect rivers and streams worldwide.

International Rivers, "Don't Dams Produce Cheap Electricity?," www.internationalrivers.org.

Advocates of hydropower often point to low energy costs as a reason to support the development of hydroelectricity in the United States and elsewhere. Relative to many other energy sources, hydropower is fairly inexpensive. Utilities can often afford to sell power generated from dams and reservoirs for less money than they require for electricity produced from fossil fuels, the sun, or the wind. No one disputes, for example, that the low electric bills of consumers in states such as Washington and Idaho exist in large part because of the massive hydroelectric dam complexes across the Snake and Columbia Rivers, which generate plenty of electricity for people in those states.

Still, it is easy to overstate the connection between the cost of electricity and the availability of hydropower. Though hydropower-rich Washington has low electricity costs, for example, residents of several other states that generate substantial amounts of hydropower pay much higher prices. California and New York, for instance, rank third and fourth among the states, respectively, in the amount of energy generated through waterpower. Despite their use of waterpower, both California and New York are among the 10 most expensive states as far as electric costs are concerned. The same is true on an international scale. Customers in Japan and Norway, two countries where hydropower is common, pay about the same for their electricity as consumers in nations like Poland and Spain, which generate little if any hydroelectricity. The connection between hydropower production and low electric costs is not as clear or consistent as advocates of hydroelectricity like to believe.

Construction Costs

But even if hydropower production invariably led to lower electric bills for consumers, hydroelectricity would still prove too expensive to be a realistic source of energy. Hydropower production carries an enormous price tag. The issue is not so much the cost of producing the energy itself: Even hydropower's detractors recognize that because waterpower is renewable, it can be produced at relatively little cost. However, this statement, while accurate, misses the point. The reality is that while a hydroelectric plant may not cost much to run, it costs an enormous amount to build. There is not much value in producing energy on the cheap if any potential savings are outweighed by heavy construction expenses.

And the expenses involved in building a hydropower plant are indeed high. "Building large dams is both costly and difficult," notes the website for an energy corporation, "making new hydroelectric plants an unattractive option for electric companies."[24] Hydroelectric dams are enormous structures that require massive amounts of material to build. Hoover Dam on the Arizona-Nevada border, for example, contains 4.5 million cubic yards (3.4 million cubic meters) of concrete—enough to build a road across the continental United States. The cost of the concrete alone, then, represents a huge investment. The price of turbines, too, can be great, along with the expense of building a plant that can convert the energy in the water into usable power. It is not possible to build a hydroelectric facility of any size without spending freely for materials and equipment.

The sheer size of the largest hydroelectric facilities also leads to very high labor costs. Hoover Dam, begun in 1931, took five years to build.

> "Building large dams is both costly and difficult, making new hydroelectric plants an unattractive option for electric companies."[24]
>
> —Duke Energy Corporation.

During much of this time there were 5,000 or more laborers actively working on the project. Mechanization has reduced the need for workers, but at the same time the scope of projects has grown considerably. Today, the demands of construction and the length of time needed to complete a hydroelectric plant combine to make labor costs far from negligible. Construction of the Three Gorges Dam in China, for example, required an estimated 250,000 workers, some of whom worked steadily on the dam for a period of nearly 20 years. Paying these workers represents a substantial expense, adding further to the overall cost of the project.

Billions of Dollars

The result is that the cost of building even a small hydroelectric plant today can be astronomical. One good example is the Gilgel Gibe II Dam across the Omo River in Ethiopia. Completed in 2010, this facility is relatively small—its capacity is just 420 megawatts, enough to provide power for only a tiny fraction of Ethiopia's population. Nonetheless, the project cost an estimated $500 million. Larger dams are much more expensive. Another Ethiopian hydroelectric plant, Gilgel Gibe III, is expected to be complete in 2013 with a capacity of 1,800 megawatts—about four times the capacity of Gibe II. This good news, however, is tempered by financial realities. In addition to being bigger and more effective than Gibe II, Gibe III has correspondingly greater costs. As of 2010 the project was expected to cost $2 billion. Citing cost overruns and questionable construction decisions, moreover, many experts believe that $2 billion will prove to be a significant underestimate.

And even a project on the scale of Gibe III is downright cheap compared to the world's largest hydroelectric stations. A proposed hydropower facility in the Asian nation of Tajikistan, for instance, would feature a dam taller than any currently in existence. The estimated cost of completing just the first stage of the project, though, is $1.4 billion. As for the massive Three Gorges Dam project in China, official figures suggest that the project will cost as much as $27 billion. However, not all observers accept the figure as accurate. As the group International Rivers

33

The Rising Cost of Dams

Even proponents of hydroelectricity admit that dams can be extremely expensive to construct. This graph shows the approximate cost of completing three major dams over a period of half a century. The trend of increased cost continues into the twenty-first century as well. According to the Chinese government, for example, the estimated cost of the Three Gorges Dam is about $27 billion, considerably above the $18 billion price tag for the Itaipu Dam. However, many experts believe that the actual cost of the Three Gorges Dam is two or even three times the official estimate.

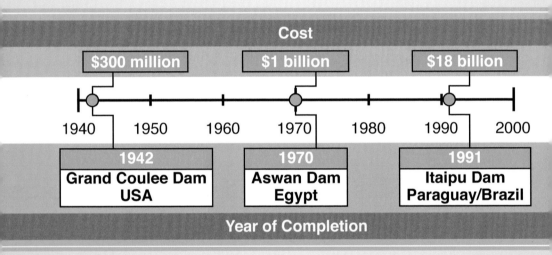

Cost

| $300 million | $1 billion | $18 billion |

1940 — 1950 — 1960 — 1970 — 1980 — 1990 — 2000

| 1942 | 1970 | 1991 |
| Grand Coulee Dam USA | Aswan Dam Egypt | Itaipu Dam Paraguay/Brazil |

Year of Completion

Source: PBS, "Building Big: Dams." www.pbs.org.

points out, "There is evidence that some costs have not been included in this figure to avoid the impression of even bigger cost overruns."[25]

China is an increasingly wealthy nation, and its government can perhaps afford such heavy expenditures. A number of other hydropower-rich countries, such as Norway and the United States, also have the necessary funds to support the building of massive dams. And certainly some well-financed private corporations in these and other nations have been eager to invest in large-scale hydropower. Still, the question of how to get funding for big hydroelectric projects persists. As the world's economy has weakened in the last several years, fewer governments and businesses have been willing and able to provide the money necessary to underwrite the costs of large hydroelectric projects.

This is particularly true of the developing world. The $500 million it took to construct Gibe II in Ethiopia represented about one-seventh of Ethiopia's entire budget for a year; Gibe III, if built as planned, would cost more than half of one year's budget. Larger dams are even more costly. The Democratic Republic of the Congo has a yearly budget of no more than $6 billion, but its plans to construct the Grand Inga dam complex on the Congo River will run at least $1 billion beyond that. These projects require plenty of funding from outside the countries themselves. In some cases the funding has been relatively easy to arrange: An Italian company, for example, underwrote much of the cost of Gibe II. An organization known as the World Bank, which provides loans and grants for developing nations, has traditionally provided funding for hydropower projects in the past as well.

Loans and Funding

But there are signs that the expense of building enormous dams is becoming harder for investors and governments to justify. During the worldwide recession that began in 2008, a number of financiers and government agencies withdrew support for various planned hydropower plants, leading to the delay or cancellation of several large projects. And though the World Bank has been a strong supporter of hydropower in the past, its policies are more and more coming under attack from scientists and business leaders who question the organization's priorities. "Small hydropower dams are more sustainable and economically viable than the large hydropower projects,"[26] points out Ugandan environmentalist Frank Muramuzi, arguing that the World Bank should shift its funding programs away from multi-billion-dollar dam facilities.

For underdeveloped countries, moreover, the hefty costs of constructing hydroelectric plants carry one further drawback. Even if a country such as Ethiopia or Tajikistan is able to obtain funding from outside sources—not a guarantee in this day and age—the money provided by other countries and corporations comes with conditions. Loans from the World Bank and most foreign governments, for example, must eventually be paid back. And though China often underwrites the initial expenses associated with dam construction in Africa, the money is not free. Instead, China exchanges the money for raw materials such as minerals—or for a share of the electricity produced by the completed hydroelectric project. This may be good for China, but it deprives the other nation of some of its most valuable resources. A country that takes the money, one observer warns, may become "China's vassal state"[27]—in effect, forfeiting its independence to become a colony for China.

> "Small hydropower dams are more sustainable and economically viable than the large hydropower projects."[26]
>
> —Ugandan environmentalist Frank Muramuzi.

Too Many Costs

Providing cheap and plentiful energy is certainly a worthy goal, and existing hydroelectric plants can play a role in attaining it. No one's interests are served, however, by pretending that hydropower is highly cost-effective. It is not. In a race to build ever bigger, higher-capacity hydroelectric plants, wealthy countries spend billions of dollars that might better be spent on other programs. Poorer nations struggle to obtain funding for projects that they could never afford on their own—and that may in the end cost them not just money they do not have and cannot afford, but their identity and autonomy as well. When startup costs, funding problems, and similar issues are factored into the equation, the price of hydroelectricity is much higher than many people think.

Chapter Three

How Does Hydropower Impact the Environment?

Hydropower Is an Environmentally Friendly Source of Energy

Compared to fossil fuels, and even to some other alternative fuel sources, hydropower is environmentally friendly. Capturing the energy of water causes much less damage to the earth than drilling for oil or mining for coal. Unlike fossil fuels, too, hydropower produces little air pollution and little carbon dioxide. And the environmental risks of hydropower accidents are far lower than the risks of oil spills, mine collapses, and nuclear plant meltdowns. No power source is completely green, but hydropower presents much less danger to the environment than most other methods.

The Debate

Hydropower Has Negative Effects on the Environment

While hydropower is renewable and does not carry the ecological risks of coal, oil, and nuclear power, its effect on the environment is far from positive. Hydroelectric dams flood millions of acres of forests and other ecosystems, killing plants and animals. Hydroelectricity also affects the environment along the river both above and below the dam, sometimes changing the temperature and salinity of the water and all too often threatening to wipe out certain species altogether. Large dams can even produce a greenhouse gas called methane. From an environmental standpoint, hydropower leaves much to be desired.

37

Hydropower Is an Environmentally Friendly Source of Energy

"We need to get back to the basics of protecting and developing the original green energy: hydropower."

—Tom McClintock, US representative from California.

Tom McClintock, "Opening Statement," US House of Representatives, March 4, 2010. http://republicans .resourcescommittee.house.gov.

The environment is a matter of much concern in the modern world. As the population grows and technology improves, the activities of people have had an increasingly negative effect on the earth. Cars and trucks spew greenhouse gases into the atmosphere, leading to climate change; urban sprawl in wealthy countries and careless logging in developing nations destroy ecosystems; industrial wastes pollute the oceans and rivers of the world. Many national and international leaders recognize the potential consequences of environmental degradation. As a United Nations scientific panel concluded in early 2012, "a complete overhaul of the way the planet is managed is urgently needed."[28]

In recent years energy use has been a leading contributor to environmental damage. Carbon dioxide, for example, is the main culprit in global climate change. According to one study, over 80 percent of the carbon dioxide produced in the United States comes from burning fuel to produce electricity, heat, and other forms of power. Similarly, energy consumption makes up a large share of air and water pollution, and the process of extracting fossil fuels from the earth can cause major environmental degradation. Coal mining can destroy mountaintops, for example, and the heavy equipment used to bring oil and natural gas to the surface can significantly scar the earth.

Not surprisingly, then, many scientists and energy experts are eager to find, expand, and develop energy sources that are more ecologically friendly than the ones most in use today. In a 2011 speech United Nations secretary-general Ban Ki-Moon called for a worldwide green energy revolution. While Ki-Moon did not single out any particular energy source in this speech, he might well have been thinking of hydropower as a major contributor to the effort. Generated from an endless supply of water, hydroelectricity does not foul the air and produces virtually no carbon dioxide. As an economic development agency called the Pacific Northwest Waterways Association puts it, hydropower is "clean, renewable, and ready when we need it."[29] From an ecological standpoint, then, hydropower makes excellent sense as an energy source for the future.

Pollution

One clear advantage of hydropower from an environmental standpoint is that it produces virtually no pollutants. "Hydropower's air emissions are negligible because no fuels are burned,"[30] notes the US Environmental Protection Agency (EPA). That is in stark contrast to the activities associated with fossil fuel use. Every coal-fired power plant sends particles into the air; every gasoline-fueled vehicle creates smoke and carbon monoxide. Indeed, where a typical coal-fired power plant in the United States generates 10,000 tons (9,071 metric tons) of sulfur dioxide each year, a hydropower facility of similar size produces virtually none. Likewise, toxins such as mercury-based compounds and nitrogen oxide—a key component in smog—are common byproducts of fossil-fuel facilities, but not of hydropower plants. Thus, replacing even a single coal-based power plant with a hydroelectric facility would keep millions of pounds of toxic chemicals from fouling the atmosphere.

> "[Hydropower is] clean, renewable, and ready when we need it."[29]
>
> —Pacific Northwest Waterways Association, an economic development agency.

Removing these chemicals from the atmosphere would be of great value. The effects of these compounds on the environment are many—and all of them are negative. Sulfur dioxide, for instance, is a major component of acid rain, which can kill trees and make lakes and rivers inhospitable to fish. Mercury and arsenic are similarly destructive. "Compounds containing mercury [are] highly toxic to . . . animals if inhaled or swallowed,"[31] the EPA points out. Switching from fossil fuels to nonpolluting hydropower, then, would have a strongly beneficial effect on the environment.

The lack of pollutants in hydropower generation has an impact on human health, too. The smog, mercury, sulfur dioxide, and other pollutants pumped into the air by coal-fired plants can cause breathing problems, heart issues, and even cancer. These effects can sicken otherwise healthy people and make those who are already sick even more vulnerable. Too often the result is needless suffering and premature death. "Particle pollution from power plants," notes the American Lung Association, "is estimated to kill approximately 13,000 people a year."[32] By switching to pollution-free hydroelectricity, then, the United States could not only help the environment itself but reduce the impact of environmental damage on its citizens.

> "Hydropower's air emissions are negligible because no fuels are burned."[30]
>
> —US Environmental Protection Agency.

Carbon Dioxide

Hydropower has another ecological advantage, too: Its contribution to greenhouse gases is insignificant. The most important greenhouse gas, and the one most clearly linked to issues of climate change, is carbon dioxide. While this compound is used by plants to create oxygen, making it is essential to the presence of life on Earth, carbon dioxide is problematic in large amounts. Along with other greenhouse gases, carbon dioxide traps heat and prevents it from leaving the atmosphere. Rising levels of greenhouse gases in recent years have increased the atmosphere's ability to retain heat, thereby raising temperatures, altering rainfall patterns, and causing other climate changes.

As with pollutants, power plants that use fossil fuels produce enormous quantities of carbon dioxide. The average American coal-fired power plant generates almost 4 million tons of carbon dioxide each year. Worldwide, fossil fuel plants give off a staggering 10 billion tons of carbon dioxide annually. Nearly all scientists agree that all this carbon dioxide is already causing massive strains on the world and its people. "Carbon emissions impose a huge cost on society by threatening the basic elements of life—access to water, food production, health and the environment," reports the Center for Global Development. "Economists have estimated these 'social costs' at anywhere from $8 per ton to as high as $100 per ton of CO_2."[33]

But although carbon dioxide is produced by fossil fuels, it is not generated in the production of hydropower. "Hydroelectric . . . facilities produce zero emissions of CO_2,"[34] notes 25x'25, an organization that studies energy policy. The implication is easy to see: If every coal-fired electrical plant across the globe were taken offline today and replaced by a clean hydropower facility, the world would not need to deal with the effects of billions of tons of new carbon dioxide every year. For the sake of the environment, a rising emphasis on hydropower in the future makes excellent sense.

A Renewable Resource

Hydropower has one final benefit where the environment is concerned. Like power derived from wind and solar sources, hydropower is renewable. Where oil and natural gas supplies are finite and will eventually run out, hydroelectricity is generated by flowing water. Unless there are dramatic and wholly unexpected changes to the earth's climate in the near future, rivers will continue to flow in the future much as they do today. Once a dam is built, the energy of the water can be harnessed with little impact on the environment. Hydropower, then, can be used for years to come without damaging the natural world.

Again, the contrast with fossil fuels is evident. Every ton of coal, every barrel of oil used to produce energy must first be extracted from the earth. As oil, gas, and coal reserves diminish, moreover, what remains will be increasingly difficult to find and to access, and the ecological cost of extracting them will only grow worse. When easily accessed fields of oil and coal begin to vanish, energy companies will need to drill deeper and dig further to find new supplies—thus causing ever greater scars on the landscape.

Hydropower Produces Minimal Greenhouse Gases

On average, the greenhouse gases generated by hydroelectric dams are dwarfed by the greenhouse gases produced by fossil fuel plants of similar size. This graphic compares the level of greenhouse gases produced by hydroelectric projects in Quebec to the levels generated by natural gas and by coal. The graphic shows that a gas-fired power plant of roughly equal capacity generates about 40 times more greenhouse gases than the hydroelectric facility. For coal, the difference is even more dramatic: A coal-fired plant in Quebec releases about 100 times more greenhouse gases into the atmosphere than a hydroelectric facility of the same size.

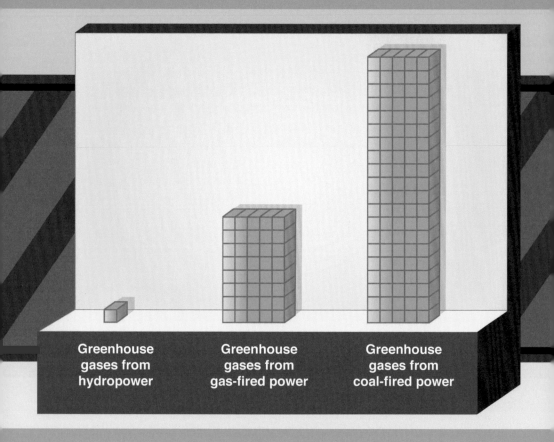

Greenhouse gases from hydropower

Greenhouse gases from gas-fired power

Greenhouse gases from coal-fired power

Note: Each square represents the annual output of greenhouse gases by a typical Quebec hydroelectric reservoir.

Source: Thierry Vandal, "Hydroelectricity: Green and Renewable," *Policy Options*, February 2012. www.irpp.org.

Positive Environmental Changes

Hydropower projects do have some impact on the natural world. A few turbines placed strategically in a river, for example, can reduce the flow of the water somewhat and may even raise the river's temperature slightly. The flooding from the creation of a reservoir can turn forests, canyons, and meadows into lakes and wetlands. Still, in most cases the construction of a dam simply exchanges one ecosystem for another. Five or ten years after the completion of a dam, the environment around it has typically adjusted, and plants, fish, and birds are thriving in the immediate area.

In the developed world, in fact, the environmental changes created by hydroelectric dams are largely positive. The lakes created by damming these rivers look clean and inviting, and many are used today for a variety of recreational purposes. Lake Sakakawea in North Dakota, for example, was created by damming the Missouri River, in part to produce hydroelectric power; it is now the site of a state park. Similarly, Lake Mead on the Nevada-Arizona border was formed when builders constructed Hoover Dam across the Colorado River; Lake Mead is today a tourist attraction offering camping, fishing, boating, and other activities. Few observers today would argue that reservoirs made from impounding water are ugly, poorly maintained, or otherwise unappealing.

Hydropower, then, is an ideal fuel for the environment. It produces little or no pollution, and it generates no carbon dioxide. Moreover, it is renewable, and its use causes minimal damage to the earth. Few energy sources are as green as hydroelectricity—or as friendly to the earth and its peoples, its animals, and its plants.

Hydropower Has Negative Effects on the Environment

"By flooding large areas of rainforest, opening up new areas to logging, and changing the flow of the water, the scores of dams being planned [in Brazil] threaten to disturb the fragile water balance of the Amazon and increase the drying of the forest."

—Aviva Imhof and Guy R. Lanza, environmental activists.

Aviva Imhof and Guy R. Lanza, "Greenwashing Hydropower," *World Watch*, January/February 2010.

While hydropower has many environmental benefits, it is much less environmentally friendly than it appears. In most cases hydroelectric production requires the building of enormous dams. The construction of a dam not only serves to hold water in place until it is needed; it can also scar landscapes, destroy ecosystems, threaten wildlife, and even increase the buildup of greenhouse gases in the atmosphere. The damage to the earth caused by the building of these massive dams is far from trivial.

Fish, Temperature, and Silt

The construction of a typical hydroelectric dam requires major changes to the river where it will be sited—and to the surrounding land as well. Most obviously, the building of a dam interrupts the flow of what was originally a freely moving river. The effect is to take one river and turn it into two barely connected sectors. This change can have enormous consequences for wildlife. In the Pacific Northwest, for example, salmon typically are born far upstream, then swim dozens or hundreds of miles down the river into the ocean. When they are ready to reproduce, the salmon swim back upstream. But by blocking the flow of the water, dams can make it impossible for the salmon to reach their destination.

In response to this issue, modern dams are usually built with special "fish ladders," a series of pools that allow the salmon to bypass the dam. Still, the ladders are not perfect. One common route for Pacific salmon, for instance, takes them up the Columbia and Snake rivers. This route, however, requires the salmon to move past eight dams and navigate eight of these ladders. Long before they reach the end of their journey, the salmon are stressed and weak. According to a recent estimate, up to 30 percent of them do not survive. Partly as a result, the number of salmon in northwestern rivers has dwindled significantly in the last several decades. "There are many factors that affect salmon throughout their life cycles," notes the website for an ecological group called Idaho Rivers United, "but the main reason for their sustained decline is dams."[35]

For some fish the problems with dams are even more severe. In many rivers hydroelectric dams present such a barrier to certain kinds of fish that these species have disappeared altogether from one part of the stream. In South America, some kinds of migrating fish have become completely absent from the upper parts of the Paraná River; environmental activists charge that the many dams along this waterway block the progress of the fish. The Chinese sturgeon, moreover, has been wiped out in several Chinese rivers that have been dammed for hydroelectricity generation. And dams along the Missouri River, reports the US Geological Survey, "have lowered populations for many river fish and bird species, some to the extent that they are [now] federal or state-listed as endangered, threatened, or species of special concern."[36]

> "There are many factors that affect salmon throughout their life cycles, but the main reason for their sustained decline is dams."[35]
>
> —Idaho Rivers United, an ecological group.

Water temperature is another example of how dividing a river with a dam can hurt wildlife. Most often, the water near the source of a river is cooler than the water near its mouth. Under natural conditions, the change in temperature is gradual. Building a dam, however, disrupts this process. The cooler water from the river's source is slowed considerably as it reaches the dam. Instead of rushing downstream as it did before the dam was constructed, it is held back and released in only small amounts. Because the colder water is not replenished regularly, the lower part of the river becomes warmer. On some rivers the increased water temperatures have stressed and even killed fish that thrive in slightly cooler water. Not only do dams increase the water temperatures beyond what is good for some species, but they also prevent the fish from moving upstream to find a spot where the temperature will be more conducive to survival.

Dividing a river carries other ecological consequences as well. One example is silt, a nutrient-rich combination of dirt, rock, and mud that is carried in the current of many rivers. In spring, when the water is high, the silt is washed downstream and is carried into nearby fields. Once the waters have receded, it remains in place and encourages plant growth. This in turn lays the groundwork for a healthy ecosystem. The construction of a dam, however, blocks the movement of silt in a river. Instead of ending up near the river's mouth, the silt typically comes to rest just upstream of the dam. Deprived of the expected nutrients, the ecosystems downstream from the dam can be seriously damaged.

Above the Dam

What takes place downstream from a dam is of concern to environmentalists. But of even more concern is what takes place above a dam. Even the smallest dams hold back (or impound) water, creating reservoirs and lakes. By necessity, this impoundment covers a certain amount of what had formerly been dry land—meadows and valleys, deserts and forests. In the case of larger dams, the size of the flooded area is astonishing. Construction of the Three Gorges Dam, for example, created a reservoir that extends 370 miles (600km)—slightly greater than the distance from Chicago to Minneapolis. The depth of the reservoir, moreover, ranges up to 300 feet (about 90m), making the water considerably deeper than Lake Erie.

The lakes created by the installations of dams often look pretty, especially in the developed world, but appearances can be deceptive. By

Dams and Environmental Damage

Dams carry significant risks to the environment. In 2011 a team of researchers at the University of Virginia carried out a study of large dams in seven countries. One part of the researchers' work involved rating the environmental impact of each dam. Team members assigned each dam a rating of positive, negative, or undetermined based on the dam's environmental effects. The study found that none of the environmental effects of the dam were positive. While a few of the effects could not be determined, the great bulk of the effects were negative. The five environmental impacts are explained below.

Fish: A positive rating indicates that the dam tended to increase the number of fish making their homes in the river, while a negative rating shows that the dam led to a decrease in the number of fish.

Biodiversity: A positive rating is given for dams that increased the variety of plant and animal species in the vicinity; a negative rating shows that the diversity of species was harmed by the dam.

Vegetation Decline: A positive rating shows that the dam did not lead to a decrease in the amount of vegetation near the dam. A negative rating means that the dam reduced the amount of vegetation in the area.

Flow Regime: This refers to the dam's effect on a river's current and at the bottom, or bed, of the stream. A positive rating shows that the dam improves the river flow, a negative rating shows that the dam interferes with the river's usual flow.

Sedimentation: This refers to the amount of mud, silt, and rock (known collectively as sediment) deposited by the river. A positive rating indicates that the dam has changed sedimentation patterns in a way that is helpful to the environment. A negative rating indicates that the new sedimentation patterns are ecologically damaging.

(+) positive effect, (-) negative effect, (?) further investigation required								
Dam Location		Zambia	Thailand	US	Pakistan	Turkey	Brazil	Norway
Environmental Impacts	Fish	–	–	–	–	–	–	–
	Biodiversity	–	–	–	?	?	–	–
	Vegetation Decline	–	–	–	–	?	?	–
	Flow Regime	–	–	?	?	–	–	–
	Sedimentation	–	–	?	–	?	–	–
Environmental Impact Analysis		-5	-5	-3	-3	-2	-4	-5

Source: University of Virginia, "Dam Problems." www.virginia.edu.

impounding millions of gallons of water, dams destroy living things and irrevocably change ecosystems, usually for the worse. Most obviously, by flooding the landscape, hydroelectric dams cover and ultimately kill flowers, trees, and grasses. Construction of the Tucurui Dam in Brazil, a relatively small hydroelectric project by modern standards, inundated about 650 square miles (about 1750 sq km) of forest—an area 10 times the size of the District of Columbia. That represents an enormous number of plants. In 1923, similarly, the Hetch Hetchy Valley in the Sierra Mountains of California was flooded by the construction of a hydroelectric dam; US representative Jerry McNerney describes the flooding as "much to the lament of environmentalists then and today."[37] In a world in which vegetation is rapidly disappearing, the loss of an additional few hundred square miles of trees and other plants is no small matter.

Other Concerns

Flooding river valleys affects animals as well. Songbirds, mice, and other animals that nest in trees or make their homes in the ground are forced to move elsewhere as the waters rise. Ideally, they would simply move up past the level of the flooding, but this is not always possible. As environmental author Patrick McCully points out, "Animals which are closely adapted to valley bottom habitats can often not survive along the edge of a reservoir."[38] The only alternative is a long cross-country trek to find a suitable place to live—a trip that many animals, especially small ones, do not survive. The reservoirs created by hydroelectric dams may be beautiful, but that beauty masks some significant environmental problems for both animals and plants.

The environmental impact of hydroelectric dams is not limited to their immediate vicinity. The plants killed by the impoundment of water settle on the bottom of the reservoir, where they slowly decay. When plant matter decays, it produces a compound called methane—a greenhouse gas that plays an important role in climate change. Though methane is much less common in the atmosphere than carbon dioxide, it has a much more powerful effect: Scientists agree that methane is 20 times more powerful than carbon dioxide in warming the atmosphere.

According to some estimates, the methane produced by hydroelectric dams accounts for as much as 4 percent of the total warming of the atmosphere attributable to human activity.

Finally, hydroelectric facilities may cause even bigger problems for the environment. Chief among these is the possibility of a dam collapse, whether because of mechanical failure or sabotage. Such a collapse would release millions of gallons of water at once; the resulting torrent would devastate the area downstream, with the environmental repercussions lasting for years. Similarly, the sheer weight of large dams has been shown to destabilize the earth and cause earthquake activity. Geologists believe, for example, that the construction of a hydroelectric dam contributed to a 2008 earthquake in the Sichuan province of China. A major earthquake brought about by a dam would cause incalculable harm to the natural world.

> "The [energy] industry's attempt to repackage hydropower as a green, renewable technology is both misleading and unsupported by the facts."[39]
>
> —Aviva Imhof and Guy R. Lanza, environmental activists.

Not an Ideal Choice

The ecological issues with hydropower, then, are clear. Far from being a benign influence on the natural world, hydropower contributes to climate change, destroys ecosystems, and harms wildlife. As environmental activists Aviva Imhof and Guy R. Lanza write, "The [energy] industry's attempt to repackage hydropower as a green, renewable technology is both misleading and unsupported by the facts."[39] For these reasons, it is not an ideal choice for the energy of the future.

Chapter Four

Can the Oceans Provide a Significant Source of Hydroelectric Power?

Oceans Represent the Future of Hydropower

Although the world's rivers still have plenty of untapped hydropower capacity, the real future of hydropower lies not in rivers but in oceans. Ocean currents, tidal surges, and wave action can all be harnessed to produce an almost infinite supply of energy. To be sure, tapping the power of the oceans is complex, but the technology to make ocean energy possible is improving each year. This technology will continue to improve as the world increasingly recognizes the benefits of ocean-generated hydropower. The oceans, then, represent the future of hydropower.

The Debate

Oceans Do Not Represent the Future of Hydropower

Tapping the oceans is not likely to ever produce much energy. Because the oceans are stormier, fiercer, and more powerful than any river, ocean turbines must be built to withstand extreme stress. To date they have generally proved too fragile. Even if technology could improve today's models, moreover, the cost could easily turn out to be prohibitive. Finally, tapping the power of currents, waves, and tides may create unanticipated environmental problems. Ocean hydropower, while a tempting idea, is not the answer to the world's energy needs.

Oceans Represent the Future of Hydropower

"Ocean power will be a whole lot smarter than continuing to build gas-fired and nuclear power plants."

—*TC Palm*, a coastal Florida newspaper.

TC Palm, "Editorial: Florida Atlantic University Researchers Wading in Atlantic Ocean for Electricity," March 27, 2009. www.tcpalm.com.

The rivers and lakes of the world hold millions upon millions of gallons of water, a small fraction of which is currently used to generate hydroelectric energy. Given the benefits of hydroelectricity, it makes sense to try to expand the number of power plants that make use of river power. But the amount of water in these rivers and lakes is dwarfed by the amount contained in the world's oceans. By one estimate, the oceans of the earth hold over 300 million cubic miles (about 1.3 billion cubic km) of water, which accounts for well over 95 percent of all the water on the planet. To tap the waters of the oceans, then, could produce an almost unlimited supply of energy for the future.

Not only do the oceans contain plenty of water, but ocean waters contain a remarkable amount of energy. Indeed, the amount of energy the oceans carry is easy to spot. While on calm days some stretches of oceans seem nearly still, the water in oceans is much more often on the move—and sometimes violently so. Waves, currents, and tides, in particular, all carry a great deal of energy. According to the DOE, the power of waves alone could generate as much as 2 million megawatts of electric power. As researcher Michael Bernitsas puts it, "If we could harness just 0.1% of the energy in the oceans, we could support the energy needs of 15 billion people"[40]—a figure more than double the population of the world today.

Tides

One of the most intriguing sources of electric power from the oceans comes from the action of tides. Caused mainly by the gravitational pull of the moon, tides cause regular and predictable changes in the level of the ocean. The height difference between the high and low tides in any given place is known as the tidal range. In several spots around the globe, such as around Tahiti in the Pacific, the tidal range is negligible; the high tide may be no more than 10 or 12 inches (25 to 30cm) above the low tide. In other parts of the world, however, the tidal range is considerably larger. Tidal ranges of 25 feet (about 8m) or more can be found in the United Kingdom, Argentina, Russia, and the United States. The world's greatest tidal range—as much as 50 feet (15m)—is found in the Bay of Fundy in eastern Canada.

> "If we could harness just 0.1% of the energy in the oceans, we could support the energy needs of 15 billion people."[40]
>
> —Michael Bernitsas, energy researcher.

The tidal range is important because the greater the difference between high and low tides, the greater the volume—and the power—of the water that rushes back and forth. Thus, the higher the tidal range, the greater the amount of energy available for capture. At the Bay of Fundy, for example, the amount of water that moves through the bay each day is greater than the flow of all the world's freshwater rivers combined—and with high and low tides just six hours apart, that water is in constant motion. Not surprisingly, then, engineers have turned their attention to tapping the tides in places where the tide range is large.

There are two basic methods of harnessing the power of the tides. One involves placing turbines in the tidal stream. These turbines are designed somewhat like windmills, with arms that turn when the tide is coming in as well as when it is going out. This method provides a steady supply of energy. The other requires the construction of dam-like objects called barrages. Barrages hold back water during the tidal surge, then release it past turbines similar to those used in river hydroelectric plants. Both methods have proved effective. Already, tidal power plants are in use in Canada, France, Russia, China, and South Korea, with others under construction around the world. As these installations demonstrate, tidal power is feasible today and will likely increase in importance. As the authors of a blog about investing in renewable energy write, "Expect this list [of tidal power plants] to grow much bigger in the future."[41]

Waves

The tides are one source of ocean energy. Waves are another. "If you have ever stood along the coast and watched the waves crash into the rocks and explode in great blossoms of white spray," writes Jerry McNerney, "you've seen the ocean's potential as an energy storage system."[42] Caused primarily by the action of the wind against the water, waves are less reliable than tides. In sheltered seas and bays they are often quite small, and even in the open ocean they may be practically nonexistent on windless days. Partly as a result, the technology for tapping the power of the waves lags behind the technology for harnessing tidal energy.

Still, wave energy has plenty of potential. Waves in many parts of the world routinely reach a height of 15–20 feet (4.5–6m) close to the coast. In these regions the waves are potent enough to make wave power plants a realistic possibility. South Africa, Australia, Scotland, and the United States, for example, all have long sections of shoreline where wave power plants make good sense. "In the Pacific Northwest alone," notes the DOE, "wave energy could produce 40–70 kilowatts per meter (3.3 feet) of western coastline."[43] Given that this coast is more than 1,000 miles (600km) long, the total potential power generation is enormous.

As with tides, there are various ways of capturing wave energy. A corporation called Ocean Power Technologies, for example, has developed a device known as a PowerBuoy. The PowerBuoy is tethered to the seafloor. As the waves pass, the device bobs up and down, collecting energy and sending it through a cable to the nearby shore. PowerBuoys have been installed in several harbors in North America and Europe. There are also ways of collecting wave energy from nearer the shore. One such method, known as the pendulor device, is essentially a large box with a flap; the waves move the flap back and forth, generating usable power.

From a technological standpoint, too, wave power works. In 2008 the world's first wave farm opened in the Atlantic Ocean near the Portuguese

Projected Increases in Ocean Wave and Tidal Power Capacity

Ocean power will be an important source of electricity in coming years. A number of proposals currently under consideration would boost the number of power stations that generate electricity from ocean tides and waves. This graph shows the projected change in tidal and wave power from 2005 to 2020 in the United Kingdom and other parts of Europe. While there is considerable variation among the countries, the overall trend is sharply upward, particularly in the United Kingdom.

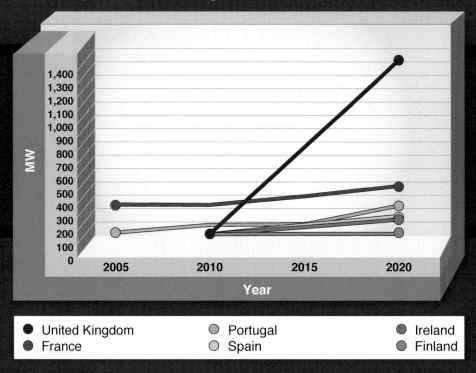

Source: RenewableUK, *Wave and Tidal Energy in the UK: State of the Industry Report*, March 2011. www.bwea.com.

coast. Admittedly, the farm was not a great success; established at the beginning of a worldwide recession, it failed to attract sufficient investors and closed after a few months of operation. But the technology worked as planned, and the plant was able to generate the electricity its builders had expected. In the following years a number of smaller-scale wave plants have been built in places as varied as California and the United Kingdom. And while wave power does not at present account for much energy production, its backers are excited about its usefulness in the future. "It is a clean and renewable energy source," sums up the web page of a wave energy company, "and its potential is huge."[44]

Ocean Currents

A third source of hydropower in the oceans comes from currents, which carry water from one part of the ocean to another. Often described as rivers within the oceans, the strongest currents are far bigger and faster than even the world's mightiest rivers. The Gulf Stream current, for example, which flows from the Caribbean Sea to Europe, has a width of up to 60 miles (96km) and a depth of about 3,000 feet (1km). In addition, it travels at double the speed of most navigable rivers. The result is a never ending supply of moving water. Every second, about 1 billion cubic feet (30 million cubic meters) of water flows past any given point along the Gulf Stream.

Not surprisingly, then, the potential of using ocean currents for energy intrigues many engineers and scientists. While there are undeniable technological issues involved in making this type of hydropower a reality, the possible payoff is vast. According to one estimate, Florida could supply about a third of its electricity needs by tapping just one-thousandth of the energy of the Gulf Stream as it flows past the state. Countries such as the United Kingdom, Italy, and Japan could also benefit enormously from harnessing the energy of ocean currents.

> "In the next few years, the wave and tidal industry will move from demonstrator machines towards substantial commercial development."[45]
>
> —Alex Salmond, a Scottish government official.

At present the capture of ocean currents for electrical power is very much in its infancy. Nonetheless, a number of scientists are hard at work devising cost-effective methods of harnessing the energy of the currents. Florida researcher Rick Driscoll, for example, is developing a method of installing rotating turbines about 1,000 feet (330m) below the surface of the ocean. Driscoll has obtained grants from the state of Florida to help him develop his plans. Similarly, an American company called Gulfstream Technologies has a plan to install turbines just below the ocean's surface, adding weights to place each turbine where the current is at its most powerful. Gulfstream Technologies, in turn, has partnered with McNeese State University in Louisiana to assist in making its devices a reality.

An Untapped Source for the Future

Though the technologies are not yet ready to generate energy from actual ocean currents, many observers expect that to change in the next few years. The same is true of other ocean power technologies. As a Scottish government official predicted in 2011, "In the next few years, the wave and tidal industry will move from demonstrator machines towards substantial commercial development."[45] The energy stored in currents, waves, and tides is simply too important to remain untapped for long.

Oceans Do Not Represent the Future of Hydropower

> "Promising sites for large scale tidal installation are rare and pose recreational and environmental problems."
>
> —25x'25, an advocacy organization that lobbies for renewable fuels in the United States.
>
> 25x'25, "Why Renewables: Hydroelectric and Tidal Power." www.25x25.org.

It would be wonderful if the oceans were a realistic source of power for human beings. For reasons involving technology, cost, and the environment, it is doubtful that the oceans will ever supply more than a tiny fraction of the world's electrical needs. One problem is that ocean energy advocates typically overestimate the amount of energy the oceans can supply. Vast stretches of coastline have insignificant tides, little wave activity, and currents that move slowly or scarcely at all. Similarly, much of the energy carried by the oceans is in open water, too far from land to be effectively transformed into electrical power. "Extraction of [tidal] energy may seem attractive," notes Dutch oceanographer Hans van Haren, "but in reality there is very little tidal energy to be had."[46]

The recent history of ocean power, moreover, is not impressive. The first modern tidal power facility opened in France in 1966, long after hydroelectric plants along rivers were commonplace. This plant, known as the La Rance station, was built at great cost and has a capacity of just 240 megawatts. This amount is far less than the river-based power plants of western Europe and not enough to increase France's energy supply in any significant way. The ocean power plants that have been established since 1966, moreover, are no more valuable. A Chinese tidal plant built to much acclaim in 1985, for example, has a capacity of just over three megawatts, and the most productive ocean plant to date, a South Korean tidal facility completed in 2011, generates only 254 megawatts. Compared to river-based hydropower plants, not to mention the electricity generated from coal, oil, and natural gas, these totals are tiny.

Technological Issues

There are good reasons for these small figures. Tapping the power of the oceans presents technological problems far beyond those presented by harnessing the energy in rivers. The oceans are huge, thousands of times larger than any river or lake, and the water frequently moves much faster than in most rivers. As a result, the turbines used even in the largest rivers are simply not suitable for use in the much harsher environment of the ocean. The power, volume, and speed of ocean waves and currents, even on ordinary days, can damage or destroy turbines made for river use. The problem is made considerably worse, too, when violent storms stir up the winds and waves.

> "Extraction of [tidal] energy may seem attractive, but in reality there is very little tidal energy to be had."[46]
>
> —Hans van Haren, oceanographer.

Thanks to extensive research and the development of better materials over the last two decades, turbines have grown stronger and more efficient, and the best of them have had some success in tapping the power of the waves and the tides. But even today's technologies are not nearly as sturdy and reliable as they need to be to withstand the harsh treatment of the ocean waters. Despite all the efforts made by Gulfstream Technologies to build a turbine that can harness offshore currents, for example, as of 2011 the company has yet to test a prototype except in fresh water. Perhaps Gulfstream and its partners will be able to build a working turbine strong enough to hold up against the oceans. It is not at all clear, however, when that day will come. And there is no guarantee that it will arrive at all.

Similarly, transferring ocean power to a place where it can be used is an issue. The energy collected by turbines placed in the waves or in a current has to be moved to onshore power plants in order to convert

In early 2012 Tom Murphy, a physicist who writes frequently on energy issues, developed a chart that rates various sources of alternative energy depending on the feasibility for the future. The chart shown here is a much simplified version of Murphy's work. Each of six energy sources is rated along five axes: *abundance*, or the amount of energy each source can realistically produce; *ease of use*, or how simple the technology is to install and maintain; *consistency*, or whether the source can be used whenever a power supply is needed; *demonstrated*, or the source's documented ability to provide energy; and *backyard*, or whether the source can be used on a small scale or even by individual property owners. This chart awards the three basic types of ocean power four greens and six blues; in comparison, the other three energy sources listed a total of nine greens and only three blues. This distribution leads to Murphy's overall conclusion that ocean power is unlikely to compete with other forms of alternative energy.

	Abundance	Ease of Use	Consistency	Demonstrated	Backyard
Ocean Power					
Tides	□	□	■	□	□
Currents	■	■	□	□	□
Waves	□	□	■	■	□
Other Alternative Fuels					
Solar	□	□	□	□	□
Traditional Hydro	□	□	■	□	■
Wind	■	□	□	□	□

▢ Performs very well	▢ Performs very poorly	▢ Neutral

Source: Tom Murphy, "The Alternative Energy Matrix," *Do the Math*, February 7, 2012. http://physics.ucsd.edu.

it to electricity. That requires cables to link the turbines with the plant. These cables need to be exceptionally strong and sturdy to avoid being damaged in the pounding waves. Corrosion of the metal in the cables, a consequence of the constantly flowing water, can stress and weaken them. Marine animals and plants may also wrap around the cables, reducing their effectiveness. Under the best circumstances, cables carrying energy from the ocean to a land-based power plant will need extensive maintenance. Even if technology made it easy to tap the power of waves and currents—which at present it does not—turning that energy into electricity would still present a huge challenge.

Costs of Ocean Power

Money is another important consideration. Building and installing turbines, barrages, and other devices to capture ocean energy carries a high price tag. The sophisticated designs of ocean turbines as compared to river-based hydroelectricity make them more costly to produce. Likewise, setting the turbines in place in a rough sea can be expensive, and maintenance in the harsh underwater environment is more costly still. To date, the costs associated with ocean power are far higher than the costs for other fuels—including solar, wind, and traditional hydropower as well as fossil fuels like oil and natural gas. That is a strong incentive for business leaders and governments to invest in these other energies rather than in trying to tap the waves, tides, and currents.

The cost disparity between ocean power and other forms of energy is not as great as it once was. Still, it remains significant. A 2010 study found that generating power from the ocean waves was about five times more expensive than producing the same amount of energy from the wind. The effects of the increased cost are easy to see. The wave farm established in Portugal in 2008, for example, did not survive for even a year. While the beginning of a worldwide recession undoubtedly contributed to the project's failure, it is also true that the startup costs were huge. Since the farm could not produce enough electricity to recoup these expenses, the farm's owners could not make money.

More recently, the United Kingdom dropped a long-standing plan to tap the tides of the Severn Estuary, second only to the Bay of Fundy in tidal range among the coastlines of the world. Though the project could have accounted for 5 percent of the UK's total electricity needs, government officials decided in the fall of 2010 not to proceed with the plan.

60

"There is no strategic case at this time for public funding of a scheme to generate energy in the Severn estuary," says Chris Huhne, the energy secretary for the UK, pointing out that the cost of the project might be as much as $50 billion. "Other low carbon options represent a better deal for taxpayers and consumers."[47] The initial expense was simply too high compared to the amount of energy that the plant could produce.

Ocean Energy and the Environment

Finally, the use of ocean power carries with it several important environmental concerns. Some of these concerns are related to wildlife. The tidal barrage planned for the Severn Estuary, for example, was opposed by several environmentalist organizations on the grounds that it would destroy valuable bird habitat and affect some rare species of fish. The constant spinning of wave turbines, moreover, has been linked to the deaths of fish that come too close to the devices; this is known as the "Cuisinart effect"[48] because of the way the fish are sliced by the whirling blades. In California, captains of commercial fishing boats have expressed concerns about possible loss of fish species due to the presence of wave turbines in marine feeding grounds.

A more serious issue, however, involves the effect of removing energy from the water. Decisions related to the environment often have unexpected and unintended consequences. Some experts worry that by harnessing the energy contained in tides, for example, power facilities will slow the flow of the water and reduce the level of the tide. In a worst-case scenario, tides in some parts of the world could virtually disappear. For scientists like van Haren, this prospect raises major concerns. "Tides are indispensable for life in shallow seas," van Haren writes. "Without them, ocean life would come to a halt. . . . What [energy] there is [in tides] comes at high ecological cost."[49]

> "There is no strategic case at this time for public funding of a scheme to generate energy in the Severn estuary. Other low carbon options represent a better deal for taxpayers and consumers."[47]
>
> —Chris Huhne, United Kingdom energy secretary.

And tapping the currents of the world's oceans could result in global environmental disaster. As with tides, harnessing a current reduces the volume and speed of the water. The Gulf Stream has carried warm water from the Caribbean to Europe for centuries. It enables Europe—most of which is further north than most of the United States—to enjoy relatively mild winters and long growing seasons. If too much energy is taken from the Gulf Stream, the current might no longer carry sufficient warm water northward to Europe, causing temperatures to plunge. "The plan is to proceed cautiously," writes one observer about the prospect of harnessing the Gulf Stream's energy, "given that the Gulf Stream moderates temperatures in the United Kingdom and Europe and impacts climate globally."[50]

A Path Not Worth Pursuit

It is unclear how much energy is too much when it comes to tapping the resources of the world's currents. Thus, ocean power raises the constant possibility of damaging environmental consequences. When these concerns are combined with technological questions and worries about excessive costs for the small amount of energy that oceans can provide, it is evident that the benefits of ocean power cannot balance the negatives—and should not justify pursuing this path in the future.

Source Notes

Overview: Visions of the Future: Hydropower

1. Arthur Fisher, "World's Largest Dam," *Popular Science*, August 1996, p. 69.
2. My Yangtze Cruise, "Three Gorges Dam." www.myyangtzecruise.com.
3. Peter H. Gleick, "Three Gorges Dam Project, Yangtze River, China," *The World's Water: 2008–2009*, p. 142.
4. Quoted in Associated Press, "Three Gorges Dam Has Caused Urgent Problems, Says China," *Guardian*, May 19, 2011. www.guardian .co.uk.

Chapter One: Can Hydropower Ever Replace Fossil Fuels?

5. REVE, "Wind Energy in China." www.evwind.es.
6. Energy Matters, "Wind and Solar Power Statistics, Facts and Trivia." www.energymatters.com.au.
7. Samuel R. Avro, "Charting the Dramatic Gas Price Rise of the Last Decade," *Consumer Energy Report*, March 14, 2012. www.consumer energyreport.com.
8. Quoted in Lee Dye, "Researcher: Dwindling Oil Supplies to Bring Energy Crisis," ABC News, February 11, 2012. http://abcnews.go.com.
9. US Energy Information Administration, *International Energy Outlook 2009*, May 27, 2009. www.eia.doe.gov.
10. Union of Concerned Scientists, "How Hydrokinetic Energy Works," 2010. www.ucsusa.org.
11. Brian Somers, "Happy Energy Independence Day!," Renewable Energy World, July 2, 2010. www.renewableenergyworld.com.
12. Ecoleaf, "Hydroelectric Powered Energy." www.ecoleaf.com.
13. Danish Energy Agency, "Climate and Energy Guide: Hydropower." www.klimaogenergiguiden.dk.
14. Alaska Center for the Environment, "Susitna Hydroelectric Project," 2008. http://akcenter.org.

15. Kristin Underwood, "Hydropower Not Likely Under New Climate Future," *Treehugger*, October 22, 2009. www.treehugger.com.

16. Quoted in International Rivers, "The World Commission on Dams Framework—a Brief Introduction," February 29, 2008. www.inter nationalrivers.org.

17. Quoted in Adam Vaughan, "London Slow to Become the 'Electric Car Capital of Europe,'" *Guardian*, February 1, 2012.

Chapter Two: Is Hydropower Affordable?

18. Christopher Hope, "Solar Panels Subsidy Was 'One of the Most Ridiculous Schemes Ever Dreamed Up,' Lord Marland Says," *Telegraph*, January 30, 2012. www.telegraph.co.uk.

19. Wisconsin Valley Improvement Company, "Facts About Hydropower." www.wvic.com.

20. Arshad H. Abbasi, "Hydropower: Clean Energy," *Dawn*, March 4, 2010. http://archives.dawn.com.

21. Chris Nelder, "The End of Fossil Fuel," *Forbes*, July 24, 2009.

22. Quoted in Duncan Clark, "Phasing Out Fossil Fuel Subsidies 'Could Provide Half of Global Carbon Target,'" *Guardian*, January 19, 2012. www.guardian.co.uk.

23. Barack Obama, "Remarks by the President in State of the Union Address," January 24, 2012. www.whitehouse.gov.

24. Duke Energy Corporation, "FAQs: Conventional Hydro." www.duke -energy.com.

25. International Rivers, "China's Three Gorges Dam," November 2009. www.internationalrivers.org.

26. Quoted in Bretton Woods Update No. 69, "Large Hydropower: Renewable or Not?," February 15, 2010. www.brettonwoodsproject.org.

27. Quoted in Andrew Higgins, "Chinese-Funded Hydropower Project Sparks Anger in Burma," *Washington Post*, November 7, 2011.

Chapter Three: How Does Hydropower Impact the Environment?

28. United Nations Environment Programme, "Overhaul of Global Environmental Governance to Meet 21st Century Challenges Tops

Emerging Issues Selected by UN Scientific Panel," February 20, 2012. www.unep.org.

29. Pacific Northwest Waterways Association, "The Role of Hydropower in the Northwest." www.pnwa.net.

30. US Environmental Protection Agency, "Clean Energy." www.epa .gov.

31. US Environmental Protection Agency, "Clean Energy."

32. Quoted in Joanna Zelman, "Power Plant Air Pollution Kills 13,000 People per Year, Coal-Fired Are Most Hazardous: ALA Report," *Huffington Post*, March 14, 2011. www.huffingtonpost.com.

33. Quoted in *Science Daily*, "Carbon Dioxide Emissions from Power Plants Rated Worldwide," November 14, 2007. www.sciencedaily .com.

34. 25x'25, "Why Renewables: Hydroelectric and Tidal Power." www .25x25.org.

35. Idaho Rivers United, "Why Salmon Are Disappearing." www.idaho rivers.org.

36. US Geological Survey, "Dams and Reservoirs on the Upper Missouri River," North Dakota Water Science Center. http://nd.water .usgs.gov.

37. Jerry McNerney and Martin Cheek, *Clean Energy Nation*. New York: AMACOM, 2012, p. 59.

38. Patrick McCully, "Flooding for Posterity." www.internationalrivers. org.

39. Aviva Imhof and Guy R. Lanza, "Greenwashing Hydropower," *World Watch*, January/February 2010.

Chapter Four: Can the Oceans Provide a Significant Source of Hydroelectric Power?

40. Quoted in Alternative Energy, "Renewable Energy from Slow Water Currents," January 8, 2009. www.alternative-energy-news.info.

41. Green World Investor, "List of Tidal Power Plants and Future Tidal Stations," March 13, 2011. www.greenworldinvestor.com.

42. McNerney and Cheek, *Clean Energy Nation*, p. 60.

43. US Department of Energy, "Ocean Wave Power," February 9, 2011. www.energysavers.gov.

44. Pelamis Wave Power, "Wave Power." www.pelamiswave.com.

45. Quoted in Severin Carrell, "Wave and Tidal Power Almost Ready for Mass Consumption, Says Alex Salmond," *Guardian*, September 27, 2011. www.guardian.co.uk.

46. Hans van Haren, "Tidal Power? No Thanks," *New Scientist*, April 3, 2010.

47. Quoted in *Renewable Energy World*, "UK Drops Massive Severn Tidal Scheme," October 18, 2010. www.renewableenergyworld.com.

48. Quoted in Joshua Arnow, "Low Velocity Hydro Power by VIVACE," Sustainability Laboratories, January 2, 2009. www.sustainabilitylabs .org.

49. Van Haren, "Tidal Power? No Thanks."

50. New England BioLabs, "Renewable Energy Mini-Reviews." www .neb.com.

Hydropower Facts

Ocean Hydropower

- Ocean currents are not as fast as strong winds, but water is at least 800 times denser than air. As a result, a current that moves at 12 miles per hour (19kph) produces the same amount of energy as a gale blowing at 110 miles per hour (177kph).
- The Agucadoura Wave Farm off the Portuguese coast was the world's first attempt to capture the energy of ocean waves on a large scale. However, it never produced more than 2.25 megawatts of electricity.
- Fish do not like to be near sound waves that travel at certain frequencies. Research suggests that if ocean turbines are designed to send out sound waves at these frequencies, fish may stay away from the turbines and keep themselves safe from the spinning blades.
- Tidal hydroelectric systems can turn about 80 percent of the potential energy in tides into power for human use. That is about 10 percent less than standard river hydropower but is considerably more efficient than fossil fuel technology.
- Oregon is one of several coastal states that offers scientists and entrepreneurs tax credits and low-interest loans to encourage wave and tidal power installations.

Hydropower in the United States

- The first modern hydroelectric plant was built along the Fox River in Appleton, Wisconsin. It began operation in 1882.
- The average dam in the United States is about 40 years old.
- About 2,400 US dams generate hydroelectricity. This amounts to only about 3 percent of the total number of dams in the nation.
- In the United States renewable energy sources account for just over 11 percent of the total electricity used nationally. However, hydropower accounts for 97 percent of this figure.

- Nearly all US states produce at least some hydropower. As of 2010 only Delaware, Rhode Island, Mississippi, and Kansas generate less than 30 megawatts of electricity from hydropower facilities.
- In 2010 the states that generated the most hydropower were, in order, Washington, California, Oregon, New York, and Montana. Washington produced slightly more hydropower than the next two states combined.
- The wild salmon population in the Pacific Northwest is currently estimated at about 300,000. In the early 1900s, the number of salmon was probably about 16 million.
- Over 300 dams have been removed in the United States since 2000, some to protect wildlife, others because they are no longer needed, and still others because they are crumbling.

Hydropower in Developing Nations

- Ethiopian officials project that the Gibe III hydroelectric complex will not only provide plenty of power for Ethiopia, but that it will also produce excess power that can be sold to other African and European countries.
- The World Bank provides approximately $1 billion each year for hydropower projects in developing countries, mainly in Africa and south and southeastern Asia.
- Africa currently has more than 1,000 large dams that generate hydropower. Even so, over 70 percent of the people living in Saharan and sub-Saharan Africa have no access to electricity.
- The Itaipu Dam on the border between Paraguay and Brazil is an interesting example of international cooperation; it is run jointly by both countries, each of which is entitled to a share of the electricity it produces.
- A hydroelectric reservoir in Suriname, South America, covers about 1 percent of the country's total territory. To cover a similar percentage of US territory would mean flooding the states of Vermont, New Hampshire, Massachusetts, Connecticut, and Rhode Island.
- About 2 million people, most of them in developing nations, are displaced every year by dam construction.

Hydropower Elsewhere

- Because Norway generates nearly all of its electricity from hydropower, and because it exports some of the energy it does not need, Norway is often known as the Rechargeable Battery of Europe.
- The five nations that produce the most hydropower are, in order, China, Canada, Brazil, the United States, and Russia.
- About 5,000 dams around the world were built before 1960.
- The Three Gorges Dam, in addition to providing electricity, has also deepened river channels, making it easier to ship goods along the Yangtze. The dam may have helped lessen the risk of flooding along the river as well.

Related Organizations and Websites

American Rivers
1101 Fourteenth St. NW, Suite 1400
Washington, DC 20005
phone: (202) 347-7550 • fax: (202) 347-9240
website: www.americanrivers.org

An advocacy organization lobbying on behalf of rivers and river systems in the United States and elsewhere, American Rivers often opposes new dam projects; it also works to mitigate the environmental problems caused by existing hydroelectric complexes.

Canadian Hydropower Association
340 Albert St., Suite 1300
Ottawa, ON, Canada K1R 7Y6
phone: (613) 751-6655 • fax: (613) 751-4465
website: www.canhydro.org

This is a trade organization that represents members of the hydropower industry in Canada, which produces more hydroelectricity than any nation but China. Much of its time and effort is spent lobbying on behalf of hydroelectric development.

Hydropower Reform Coalition
1101 Fourteenth St. NW, Suite 1400
Washington, DC 20005
website: www.hydroreform.org

The Hydropower Reform Coalition is dedicated to changing the way hydropower plants are designed and inspected. Its particular focus is on improving the health of rivers.

Hydro Research Foundation
25 Massachusetts Ave. NW, Suite 450
Washington, DC 20001
phone: (303) 674-5254
website: www.hydrofoundation.org

This foundation advocates for governmental policies that encourage hydropower development. One of its main goals is educating people about the benefits and advantages of waterpower.

International Rivers
1847 Berkeley Way
Berkeley, CA 94703
phone: (510) 848-1155 • fax: (510) 848-1008
website: www.internationalrivers.org

This organization's focus is the protection of rivers and their ecosystems, along with advocating for the rights of people who live along riverbanks in the developing world. The group often, though not always, opposes large-scale dams and hydroelectric projects.

National Hydropower Association
25 Massachusetts Ave. NW, Suite 450
Washington, DC 20001
phone: (202) 682-1700 • fax: (202) 682-9478
website: www.hydro.org

This nonprofit organization consists of private companies and public utilities that manufacture and sell hydropower. It advocates for policies that support and encourage hydropower use.

United States Department of Energy
1000 Independence Ave. SW
Washington, DC 20585
phone: (202) 586-5000 • fax: (202) 586-4403
website: www.energy.gov

This department of the US government sets energy policy. It gathers and provides information about different energy sources and the US energy supply.

Wisconsin Valley Improvement Company
2301 N. Third St.
Wausau, WI 54403
phone: (715) 848-2976 • fax: (715) 842-0284
website: www.wvic.com

This company maintains and operates more than 20 hydroelectric complexes along the Wisconsin River.

For Further Research

Books

Stephen Currie, *Hydropower*. San Diego: ReferencePoint, 2011.

Ron Fridell, *Earth-Friendly Energy*. Minneapolis: Lerner, 2009.

Michael Hiltzik, *Colossus: The Turbulent, Thrilling Saga of the Building of Hoover Dam*. New York: Free Press, 2011.

Stuart A. Kallen, *Renewable Energy Research*. San Diego: ReferencePoint, 2011.

Marilyn Nemzer, Deborah Page, and Anna Carter, *Energy for Keeps: Creating Clean Energy from Renewable Resources*. Tiburon, CA: Energy Education Group, 2010.

Periodicals

Arshad H. Abbasi, "Hydropower: Clean Energy," *Dawn*, March 4, 2010.

Associated Press, "Three Gorges Dam Has Caused Urgent Problems, Says China," *Guardian*, May 19, 2011.

Lee Dye, "Researcher: Dwindling Oil Supplies to Bring Energy Crisis," ABC News, February 11, 2012.

Aviva Imhof and Guy R. Lanza, "Greenwashing Hydropower," *World Watch*, January/February 2010.

Chris Nelder, "The End of Fossil Fuel," *Forbes*, July 24, 2009.

Renewable Energy World, "UK Drops Massive Severn Tidal Scheme," October 18, 2010.

Hans van Haren, "Tidal Power? No Thanks," *New Scientist*, April 3, 2010.

Websites

China Three Gorges Project (www.ctgpc.com.cn/en/). Provides information on China's Three Gorges Dam. Includes descriptions of the benefits it provides and a recap of its history.

Hydroelectric Powered Energy, Ecoleaf (www.ecoleaf.com/green _energy/hydroelectricpower.html). Basic information about the hydropower industry and the benefits and problems hydroelectricity presents.

Hydroelectric Power: How It Works, USGS Water Science for Schools (http://ga.water.usgs.gov/edu/hyhowworks.html). Describes the science behind hydropower, using diagrams and other visuals. Intended mainly for students.

TVA Kids.com (http://tvakids.com). This site includes student-friendly information on hydroelectricity and energy issues. It belongs to the Tennessee Valley Authority, an agency that has constructed many hydroelectric dams in the southern United States.

Wave Power, Pelamis Wave Power (www.pelamiswave.com/wave-power). Pelamis is a company involved in tapping the energy of the oceans. This site provides a useful overview of wave power and its potential.

Index

Note: Page numbers in boldface indicate illustrations.

electricity
  hydropower and cost of, 25–26,
    31–32
  hydropower as percentage of
    total global demand, 9
  measurement of, 7
  potential amount of, produced
    from wave energy, 51
electric vehicles, 17, 23
energy
  costs of, by source, **27**
  renewable energy as percentage
    of global supply, 18
  See also electricity; renewable
    energy
Environmental Protection Agency
  (EPA), 39, 40

fossil fuels
  depletion of, 13–14
  government subsidies for, 30
  hydropower as alternative to,
    14, 16–17, 18, 22–23
  power plants and
    carbon dioxide emissions
      from, 40–41
    percent of US carbon dioxide
      emissions from, 38
    pollution from, 39–40

Geological Survey, US, 45
Gilgel Gibe III Dam (Ethiopia),
  16
  cost of, 35

global warming, from methane
  produced by dams, 48–49
Goodstein, David, 14
governments, role of, in
  developing hydroelectricity,
  29–30
Grand Coulee Dam (WA), 7, **34**
Grand Inga Dam (Democratic
  Republic of the Congo), 9, 16,
  35
greenhouse gases
  emissions from coal-fired plants,
    39
  emissions from hydropower
    versus gas-/coal-fired power
    plants, **42**
  methane as, 48–49
Gulf Stream, 62
Gulfstream Technologies, 56, 58

habitat destruction
  from dams/reservoirs, 10, 48
  from tidal barrages, 61
Hetch Hetchy Valley (CA), 48
Hoover Dam, 32–33, 43
Huhne, Chris, 61
hydropower
  costs of, 21
    can provide low cost electricity
      to consumers, 25–26
    compared to other energy
      sources, 13–14, **27**
    facilities are expensive to
      build, 29, 32–35, **34**

76

About the Author

Stephen Currie has published books on topics ranging from exploration and math to goblins and pianos. He has also taught at levels from kindergarten to college. He makes his home in New York, the state that as of 2012 ranks fourth nationally in hydropower production.